"Every once in a while, it's good to take a fresh look at some of our well-worn assumptions about what Jesus is recorded as saying in the Gospels. Sometimes this involves scraping off the interpretive layers we may have been using to cover up things we wish weren't there. Andy Angel does just that by exposing afresh Jesus' words about judgment and obedience, allowing them to question—and deepen—our understanding of the God-with-us of grace and love. Working his way thoroughly and systematically through the Gospel of Matthew, Angel explores what kind of teacher Jesus really was. He challenges readers to re-examine their attitude to five 'dirty words' that are central to Jesus' teaching: authority, teaching, obey, command, and judgment. Taking these words seriously requires communities of believers to exercise humility, kindness, gentleness, and forgiveness with a new resolve. They give a Spirit-propelled momentum and energy to following Christ in the way of holiness that is good news because it is a way that changes lives. Read this book and allow your relationship with Jesus to be challenged and deepened."

—**Eeva John**
Enabling Officer for the Conversations on the Teaching Document on Human Sexuality for the House of Bishops of the Church of England

"This fresh, provocative book argues powerfully that the popular understanding of Jesus as one who welcomes us with open arms and expects little change from us is deeply and fatally flawed. Not only that, this view of Jesus is dangerous to people's lives and their standing with God. Dr Andy Angel leads us thoughtfully through Matthew's Gospel to see why this is so, and what the real Jesus is like—a Lord who teaches, encourages, and supports believers to walk with him and be transformed as they follow him humbly and obediently. Read and act on it!"

—**Steve Walton**
Professor of New Testament, Trinity College, Bristol

"How we have needed this book! On almost every page a powerful word leaps out putting succinctly the truth we have avoided for so long. This is a prophetic challenge to a church culture that so often ignores Jesus' words on judgment and finds them unacceptable. Andy takes us carefully through the teaching. Then he demonstrates how Jesus, as one always alongside us, with both gentleness and humility, teaches us to be fully obedient disciples, those who will joyfully stand on the day of judgment. Who would not want this!"

—**Graham Dow**
Assistant Bishop in the dioceses of Chester and Manchester, former Bishop of Carlisle

"Few topics are as difficult to negotiate as Jesus' teachings on judgment and forgiveness. Yet Andy Angel has produced a remarkably accessible book that shows how these teachings fit together. I especially appreciate Angel's informed reading of Matthew's Gospel, and his genuine, pastoral concern that Christians reflect the Lord Jesus in their lives and communities. He convinces us that the Jesus we think we don't want to know—who preaches obedience and judgment, forgiveness, and grace—is actually the Jesus we really need and have really wanted to know all along."

—**Elizabeth E. Shively**
Senior Lecturer in New Testament Studies, St. Mary's College, University of St. Andrews

"In this challenging book, Andy Angel persistently makes us listen to Jesus' teaching on judgement, and therefore on holiness, deeply seriously. He rightly makes us re-look at the ease with which we slide into both 'cheap grace' and 'love as a feeling' rather than the truth of costly grace and love being obedience. I echo his own words and encourage us to keep discovering that *'Living with Jesus as my teacher has been exhausting, frustrating, nerve-wracking and, time and time again, has stretched me beyond anything I thought I could manage, but it has been great.'*"

—**Paul Butler**
Bishop of Durham, UK

"Andy was one of my New Testament lecturers and he would often teach the Gospels with a tear in his eye. In this book, he guides us through the words of Jesus in the Scriptures, and endeavors to match the Jesus we encounter there with the Jesus we've constructed and interpreted in our minds. This is a richly theological book but not just that; it is a book about devotion, obedience and discipleship; encouraging us to take Jesus at his word. Jesus is too holy and too kind to leave us with our watered-down versions of himself."

—**Ben Woodfield**
Church Planter, The Antioch Network, Manchester Diocese, UK

"Who would have thought that the grace of God could become an idol? Well, not the grace itself, but, as Andy Angel points out with cutting insight, a doctrine of grace that takes the place of that love for Jesus which, according to Jesus himself, requires obeying his commandments. For a long time, I have felt that the hallowed *sola*, 'by faith alone,' has been subverted into a subtle mechanism for avoiding Paul's own insistence that the gospel is not there merely to be believed but to be *obeyed*, with what he twice calls 'the obedience of faith.' Paul and James are in full agreement, precisely because (naturally) they agree on the teaching of Jesus himself. And it is that teaching, and its central place in what it means to be a disciple, and to make disciples, that Andy Angel so effectively explores in this book. If Jesus truly is Lord as well as Savior (and what else is the essence of the gospel?), then it is at our peril (seriously) that we ignore Christ's words about judgment, and fail to do as well as to hear. Yet Andy's purpose is not merely to correct this imbalance in contemporary cultural Christianity (in the West at least), but to encourage a better and wiser and more honest pastoral practice. It's a word that needs to be heard and heeded."

—**Christopher J.H. Wright**
Langham Partnership

"Every time a new Anglican minister is licensed, they make an oath exhorting them to 'proclaim afresh the faith to each new generation.' This worthy aim is potentially undermined if the proclamation so panders to cultural context that faith itself is undermined in the re-telling. In this super book, Andy exhorts us to look afresh at some of the hard sayings of Jesus that are precisely the ones ignored or distorted in order to make the faith appear more commendable. It is a challenging but essential read if we are faithfully to preach the gospel as Jesus delivered it."

—**Richard Jackson**
Bishop of Lewes, UK

"There is a perennial danger—even among Christians—of seeing Jesus of Nazareth as the epitome of kindness but ultimately someone bland. For the Gospels and the broader New Testament tradition, on the other hand, there is something vital and visceral at stake in the life and ministry of Jesus. In his most recent book, Andy Angel brings his considerable knowledge of Second Temple Jewish apocalyptic traditions, as well as his experience as teacher and pastor to bear in situating Jesus within traditions of Torah interpretation, and exploring the difficult dimensions of the gospel that are precisely its very life."

—**Séamus O'Connell**
Professor of Sacred Scripture, St Patrick's College, Maynooth

"Andy Angel's new book is direct in its approach and broad in its scholarship. Jesus the teacher is re-presented in his context. Jesus' teaching on practical holiness is reiterated with vigor and challenge. Drawing in particular on Matthew's Gospel, Andy addresses the difficult question of judgment and how it relates to Jesus' authority as teacher. Overall the book is a tour de force that goes to the heart of who Jesus is and his message."

—**Tim Dakin**
Bishop of Winchester

The Jesus You *Really* Didn't Know

The Jesus You *Really* Didn't Know

Rediscovering the Teaching Ministry of Jesus

ANDY ANGEL

CASCADE *Books* • Eugene, Oregon

THE JESUS YOU *REALLY* DIDN'T KNOW
Rediscovering the Teaching Ministry of Jesus

Copyright © 2019 Andy Angel. All rights reserved. Except for brief quotations in critical publications or reviews, no part of this book may be reproduced in any manner without prior written permission from the publisher. Write: Permissions, Wipf and Stock Publishers, 199 W. 8th Ave., Suite 3, Eugene, OR 97401.

Cascade Books
An Imprint of Wipf and Stock Publishers
199 W. 8th Ave., Suite 3
Eugene, OR 97401

www.wipfandstock.com

PAPERBACK ISBN: 978-1-5326-4492-4
HARDCOVER ISBN: 978-1-5326-4493-1
EBOOK ISBN: 978-1-5326-4494-8

Cataloguing-in-Publication data:

Names: Angel, Andrew R., author.

Title: The Jesus you *really* didn't know : rediscovering the teaching ministry of Jesus / Andy Angel.

Description: Eugene, OR: Cascade Books, 2019 | Includes bibliographical references and index.

Identifiers: ISBN 978-1-5326-4492-4 (paperback) | ISBN 978-1-5326-4493-1 (hardcover) | ISBN 978-1-5326-4494-8 (ebook)

Subjects: LCSH: Matthew—Criticism, interpretations, etc. | Jesus Christ—Teachings | Holiness | Ethics in the Bible

Classification: BS2555.52 A54 2019 (paperback) | BS2555.52 (ebook)

Manufactured in the U.S.A.   09/05/19

To Dad

Contents

Acknowledgments | ix
Abbreviations | x

1 Personal Introduction | 1
2 The Elephant under the Carpet | 9
3 The Jesus We Don't Want to Know | 23
4 The Jesus You Didn't Know—*Really?* | 72
5 Five (Dirty) Words Every Christian Needs to Learn | 88
6 Riding the Elephant | 112
Appendix: Thoughts on Jesus, Paul, and the Law | 119

Bibliography | 133
Index of Ancient Sources | 139
Index of Modern Authors | 149

Acknowledgments

I would like to thank my father, Gervais Angel, for that conversation we had in the kitchen while washing up so many years ago. We were talking about who Jesus was and what he did. We had chatted about Jesus as Messiah, Son of God, Savior, Lord, and (most probably at length) Son of Man. We had spoken about how these different understandings of Jesus play out in the life and worship of churches today. Suddenly my father broke off into new territory asking about Jesus as teacher, or "rabbi." He asked me what I thought the church might look like if we spoke more often about Jesus as teacher. I suggested he wrote a book. He suggested I wrote one. That conversation was back in the 1980s but the question has remained with me over the years. In many ways, this book is the result of that conversation, so I want to thank my father for raising the question and with it my interest.

Many thanks are also due to the friends and colleagues who kindly read and commented on the draft of the book. Particular thanks must go to Gervais Angel (again!), Tom Coopey, Celia Davis, Tom Davis, Isabelle Hamley, Martin Hesford-Duckworth, Diane Kutar, Suse McBay, June McLellan, Isaac Pain, Sam and Thea Pearce, and Marcus Throup for your insightful comments, your encouragements, your questions and suggestions. I hope I have listened wisely and made the necessary changes for the benefit of the reader. I would also like to thank the Tyndale Fellowship New Testament study group and the Synoptic Gospels seminar of the British New Testament Conference who have heard papers on this topic and encouraged me to complete the study and publish. Your encouragement got me round to doing this in the end. I would also like to thank the team at Cascade/Wipf and Stock who have been, as always, incredibly helpful.

Abbreviations

'Abot R. Nat.	Abot de Rabbi Nathan
Ag. Ap.	Josephus, *Against Apion*
Ant.	Josephus, *Jewish Antiquities*
CD	Cairo Genizah copy of the Damascus Document
Col	Colossians
1 Cor	1 Corinthians
2 Cor	1 Corinthians
Dan	Daniel
Deut	Deuteronomy
Did.	Didache
1 En.	1 Enoch
Eph	Ephesians
Exod	Exodus
Ezek	Ezekiel
Gal	Galatians
Gen	Genesis
Hos	Hosea
Isa	Isaiah
Jas	James
Jer	Jeremiah
J.W.	Josephus, *Jewish War*
2 Kgs	2 Kings
LAB	Liber antiquitatum biblicarum (Pseudo Philo)
Lev	Leviticus
2 Macc	2 Maccabees

Abbreviations

3 Macc	3 Maccabees
4 Macc	4 Maccabees
Matt	Matthew
Mic	Micah
m. 'Abot	Mishnah, 'Abot
m. B. Qam.	Mishnah, Baba Qamma
m. Ber.	Mishnah, Berakot
m. Demai	Mishnah, Demai
m. Giṭ	Mishnah, Giṭṭin
m. Ḥag.	Mishnah, Ḥagigah
m. Ḥul.	Mishnah, Ḥullin
m. Ma'aś	Mishnah, Ma'aśerot
m. Pesaḥ	Mishnah, Pesaḥ
m. Sanh.	Mishnah, Sanhedrin
m. Ta'an.	Mishnah, Ta'anit
m. Yad.	Mishnah, Yadayim
m. Yoma	Mishnah, Yoma
Moses	Philo, *On the Life of Moses*
Neh	Nehemiah
Num	Numbers
Phil	Philippians
Ps	Psalm
Prov	Proverbs
1QS	Rule of the Community
Rev	Revelation
Rom	Romans
Sib. Or.	Sibylline Oracles
Sir	Wisdom of Ben Sira/Sirach
Spec. Laws	Philo, *On the Special Laws*
1 Thess	1 Thessalonians
2 Thess	2 Thessalonians
1 Tim	1 Timothy
2 Tim	2 Timothy
Tob	Tobit
Wis	Wisdom of Solomon
y. Šabb.	Jerusalem Talmud, Šabbat
Zech	Zechariah

I

Personal Introduction

Perhaps at this point I ought to confess some of my motivations. As with many others who put finger to keyboard, I write from a personal interest. I have a passion for holiness. I may not be very good at holiness, but I try and I want to get better. I love purity, I love goodness, I love gentleness, I love grace, I love honesty, I love authenticity, I love transparency, I love worship, I love commitment to Christ and his love. When I meet other Christians who share these passions and display these virtues, I want to spend time in their company. There is something beautiful about them and being with them is quite simply enjoyable. They manifest holiness and this makes them the most amazing people to be with. Their lives reflect the life of the Lord they serve and this is what makes them such beautiful people. I have a taste for holiness because it makes life better and because I have some experience of how unholiness destroys.

I was a cathedral chorister from the ages of ten to fifteen and sang in a choir where there was sexual abuse of choristers, which the cathedral staff at the time did not address. To me at that age it felt like preserving the beauty of the music was more important to the dean and chapter than keeping children safe, ensuring justice was done, and that those who were damaged received the help they needed. I have since forgiven the man who harmed me (and I pray for him), but I have not been able to do this without working through the heartache, the shame, the rejection of myself, and the inability to relate to others (especially my peers) that his action caused. I am now an Anglican priest working in a Church of England diocese that has been under scrutiny recently for sexual abuse by priests in the diocese and is now working hard to keep people safe from abuse. I know many others have suffered similarly and in many other institutions within society, both here and around the world. I can only be glad that Jesus did not come to whitewash over our sins with a paper-thin idea of "forgiveness" but to *sort us out*—to forgive us all we have done wrong, and then to deal with our sins root and branch as he teaches us how to live out his commandments. I can only be glad that he teaches us to treat each other with the highest respect, and to help each other stay far away from sin as we learn to live constructive, life-giving lives of holy love.

Furthermore, I write as someone who lives in one of the richest countries in the world and serves in churches where we seek God's blessing on our lives. I have attended many churches in my life, but the one that has left the longest lasting impression on me was the wonderful small Anglican fellowship in a shanty town (Pamplona Baja in Lima) that I attended aged eighteen when doing some volunteer work in Peru. A personal financial problem in the churches where I currently serve is redundancy (with the legally required payout) and working out how to continue things like mortgage payments. A personal financial problem in Pamplona Baja was not being able to earn enough money working ten hours a day to feed all your children and having to work out what to do. Something that occasionally still reduces me to tears is that we are all Christians and yet those of us in the wealthy world find it challenging to give even the 10 percent Jesus commanded us to give (Matt 23:23) to further the work of the church in, amongst other things, relieving the poverty of our brothers and sisters around the world. I have sat in too many meetings where churches, theological colleges, and other Christian organizations in the "first world" complain of lack of resources. I confess that sometimes I have lost patience and recited internally God's words through the prophet, "I hate, I despise your festivals, . . . take away from me the noise of your songs, . . . but let justice roll down like waters, and righteousness like an ever-flowing stream" (Amos 5:21–24). I have even written to a former Archbishop of Canterbury asking him to rebuke the Church of England for not tithing and instead seeking money to prop up itself, its dioceses, and its institutions when there is so much financial need in the majority world. I got a lovely letter back but with a refusal to take such action. Personally, I long for the day when all

Personal Introduction

churches (but especially those in wealthy countries) give not just their tithe but all that they are really able to give for the work of Christ in this world.

At about seventeen years of age, I got bored with church. I loved the music and I enjoyed most things from Allegri through to contemporary worship music, provided we avoided some of the less agreeable Christian folk songs of the seventies. I loved the Bible. I had read it cover to cover five or six times by then. I enjoyed intelligent sermons. I had experienced and found valuable things in pretty much most expressions of Christian worship, from high Anglicanism to the wilder forms of Pentecostalism, but still there was something missing. I had learned the value and joy of prayer and it was in prayer that I discovered what was missing from my Christian life: the challenge of change. I had learned how to enjoy God in many different musical, devotional, and liturgical expressions. I had learned many different ways of experiencing the love of God, from being rapt within that sense of transcendence in exuberant worship through to the stillness of God's presence in meditation. I had given over my life to God, but I had not yet been ready for deep, lifelong, transformative change. For me it began with learning to live differently, with no longer living out the emotions and patterns of behavior that abuse had fixed inside of me. Living with Jesus as my teacher has been exhausting, frustrating, nerve-wracking, and time and time again has stretched me beyond anything I thought I could manage, but it has been great.

I guess that I have been bitten by the bug. One of the most transformative experiences has been learning to love my neighbor *as myself*. Abuse leaves us much more able to denigrate ourselves and avoid ourselves than to love or even acknowledge ourselves. Learning to love myself, however, has not proven the greatest love of all. That is surely the love that God the Father and the Son have shared with humanity, that led the Son to die in our place on the cross (Mark 10:45) and that leads the Spirit to pour this love into our hearts (Rom 5:5). However, learning to love myself has enabled me to enjoy being the person God created me to be and to understand better how to love others. Realizing how learning to live Jesus' way could make such a difference to my life makes me want to work with God on living the life of obedient holiness that will bring greater blessing to the lives of others —and show God the love he deserves.

These are a few of the reasons I have a passion for holiness—at least, they were the first to come to mind as I put fingers to keyboard. I do not like the idea that our unholiness, that my unholiness, hurts others. Whether the hurt be physical, emotional, and personal or economic, political, and international, our sins damage lives. If we have any understanding of the love of God for anyone other than ourselves, we ought to weep over our sins and long to be changed. And if we have any understanding of the love of God, we will love others and not just ourselves, because the love of God is not selfish in the same way as our love of ourselves can so often be. If we love others, we want to do them good not harm—and that means we will want to live the way Jesus teaches us to live, for his is the way of love. Hence my passion for holiness.

But my motivation has not only been my personal passion for holiness. There has also been a pastoral concern. Someone I love very dearly once told me that she had just met a number of people from her cell group at church at Alcoholics Anonymous. They went to church to worship God. They went to the cell group because that is where the church told them that they could share close Christian fellowship. They went to Alcoholics Anonymous because that is where they were learning how to put their lives back together. Twelve-step programs like Alcoholics Anonymous use something like the class system invented by the Anglican minister and founder of Methodism John Wesley (1703–91). The class system was the precursor to contemporary Christian home groups, Bible study groups, cell groups, pastorates, and so on. When this lady told me where she was really going for fellowship, my heart sank. Not because she was attending Alcoholics Anonymous—they do a wonderful work. Rather, because the church has moved so far away from the vision Wesley and others had in creating small groups as a way of helping Christians support each other to grow in holiness. I am deeply concerned that Christian fellowship in many places has lost the depth and quality of genuine, committed, loving, and faithful friendship into which the Lord Jesus invites us as a way of life. I would love to see such fellowship grow and thrive in Christian churches—and I am convinced that where we open ourselves us to the instruction of Jesus our teacher, and we learn together from him in humility and grace, we find ourselves living this way.

I do not expect the following two chapters of this book to make particularly comfortable reading. In order to explore how practically we can grow in the beauty of holiness, I need first to identify an elephant in the room, grab it by the tusks, and then wrestle with it. By and large, when there are elephants in rooms, they are visible to all and everybody knows they are there. However, and for whatever reason, nobody wants to admit they are

Personal Introduction

there, so they all tacitly agree not to acknowledge them. Some elephants are different. Everybody knows they are there and has felt the discomfort of their presence. So, somebody has taken action and tried to sweep the elephant under the carpet. The elephant I wish to tackle is of this kind.

At the heart of much Christian discipleship lies a bundle of contradictions focused around freedom and morality. We hear the language of love and grace. We are told that God loves us unconditionally. God accepts us and welcomes us just as we are, no matter what we have done. We hear that Jesus is different from other teachers of his day. They demanded high moral standards and heaped up commandments that were impossible to bear—then or now. Jesus simply came with love and offered us the way to a new sort of faith, one of freedom and grace.

Sometime into our Christian journey, we start to read the Bible. We discover a very different Jesus in the Gospels. He talks of judgment. He warns people of a day when God will judge the world. He says that on that day he will disown anyone who was ashamed of him. He tells whole communities that they will suffer dire punishment for not listening to him. He gives some grisly pictures of eternal punishment. We read his moral demands in places like the Sermon on the Mount and wonder if Jesus really meant it—and if he did, where on earth that leaves us. Or more to the point, where in heaven or hell that *will* leave us.

We wonder how the loving Jesus who preaches grace fits with the stern Jesus who preaches judgment. We hear sermons that tell us that Paul preached grace through all Jesus did on the cross and we read this in his letters like Romans. But we notice that the same Paul warned Christians not to behave badly because one day they would stand before the judgment seat of Christ and that each of us will be accountable to God on that day. All the same, the preaching we hear and the books we read talk of grace, love, and acceptance.

Some of us find this comforting and easy. When we read the Bible, we simply edit out in our minds all the bits about judgment. We note that preachers and teachers do this. We read books by erudite biblical scholars where they do this too. So, we conclude, not unreasonably, that we can do it if they do. Some of us do this daily, and skip all the awkward sayings of Jesus and the bits of Paul that do not seem like Paul (where he speaks of judgment on Christians rather than the grace we love to hear about). Many parts of the Bible remain puzzling but, for whatever reason, we are not too worried about working the puzzle out. After a while, we find it quite easy to live with the bump the elephant makes in the carpet.

Others of us find this more disconcerting. The carpet ought to lie flat on the floor. Instead, part of it sits over three meters high in the room and occasionally raises a trunk we do not expect a carpet to have. We cannot ignore what feels like a glaring contradiction. Nor can we ignore the fact that it is not all that easy to call it a contradiction either. The Jesus who talks of God forgiving us talks of his not forgiving us in the same breath (Matt 6:14). In just one verse, Paul talks both of God's kindness towards us and of his possibly cutting us off (Rom 11:22). Jesus and Paul clearly thought *both* that God gave us grace *and* that God might judge us for doing wrong. If they could hold these two things together, then how did they hold them together? And how did this shape their spirituality? What might we learn from them? We find ourselves wanting to look underneath the carpet and make friends with the elephant that has been swept there.

In this book, I try to pick up the carpet and free the elephant. I want to take a good hard look at it in order to try to understand it better. Having done so, I want to learn to ride it. To do this, we are going to need to explore the uncomfortable topics of Jesus and judgment, and Jesus' moral teaching in some detail. We are going to need to look at some of his sayings that rarely get preached and that many of us skip over all too easily when we read the Gospels. We are going to need to work out whether some of the preaching myths like "Jesus came to bring us love instead of legalism" stand up to scrutiny or whether the Gospels say something really very different. In doing all this, I hope we get a fuller understanding of Jesus and his work in us. I hope that by the end of the book, we will find that actually we knew the uncomfortable Jesus we read of in the Gospels all along and that we also knew something of his answer to our fears.

Friends and colleagues who have kindly read the first draft have gently suggested to me that I encourage my readers as the following two chapters are spiritually quite hard, not least because they explore some of the more uncomfortable things Jesus said and thus feel quite stark. They have urged me to say some encouraging stuff before chapter 4, where the good news of this book really takes off. So, may I suggest that if you find chapters 2 and 3 hard going that you simply skip to chapter 4 and read on from there. You can come back to face the difficulties presented in these first two chapters when you have read about all Jesus does in and for us to solve these problems. Sometimes it is easier to hear the truth (in all its challenging

Personal Introduction

technicolor) when we already know the answers. If you do skip to chapter 4, do please come back to chapters 2 and 3 later as the myth-busting in these chapters helps those of us brought up on a diet of "Jesus loves us and saves us and that's pretty much all there is to it" to come to terms with what Jesus *actually* taught, and so come to know him better.

Similarly, these friends and colleagues have said that the discussion of Jesus and the law is quite long. I find myself in a catch-22 here. My argument relies on studying every single possible text that someone might use to say that Jesus either broke the law or encouraged others to do the loving thing instead of being legalistic. If I do not, then someone will say "Ah, but what about *that* text? Surely that one proves you wrong." So, missing texts out is not much of an option. However, covering every single text does mean that the section on "Jesus and the Pharisees" is long. If you are willing to believe what I am writing on the basis of a few texts, then you can skip much of the material in subsections "Breaking the Law," "Did Jesus break the Law?" and "Did Jesus teach others to break the Law?" and just read the closing paragraph of each section, which gives a summary of the section. Just remember that if you think I did not cover something, you will need to read the whole section to check whether I did or not.

In order to explore the things that I mention above, I am taking my material primarily from the Gospel of Matthew. There are two reasons that I do this is. I believe (and try to show through the chapters of this book) that Matthew tries to answer the problem of the judgment of God through writing his gospel. Second, some discussions are already quite long for the kind of book I have tried to write. Including all the relevant material from Mark, Luke, and John would have made this into a very different sort of book, and one that was far less accessible.

Finally, I am more than aware that there are numerous scholarly works that cast aspersions on the historical reliability of at least some Matthew's material and that take as axiomatic that Matthew writes to disagree with certain of his Jewish contemporaries, and so puts something of a slant on the events and characters he presents. I am writing from the standpoint that the Gospels are historically reliable documents and that Matthew presents a reliable portrait of Jesus. Those who take a different view can consider my argument as the theology of the creative redactor of gospel traditions whose work in church traditions received the title "According to Matthew." Readers on either side of the historical-reliability fence may read, I hope profitably, of the work of the risen Christ amongst his disciples in the following pages. My prayer is that this risen Christ will teach us all his ways and so take each one of us deeper into the life of worship and beauty of holiness.

2

The Elephant under the Carpet

Judgment is a problem. It does not go down well in many contemporary Western churches. We prefer a gospel of love and grace. Reading the world as broken, we want a gospel that will bring reconciliation rather than punishment. The picture of God as an absolute monarch seated upon his kingly throne deciding the fate of sinners does not appeal to many today. For a start, we prefer not to think of people as sinners. They lead broken lives. Life dealt them the kind of hand that meant they were likely to have difficulties. Poverty, lack of opportunity, abuse—and many other problems—shaped the way these people ended up behaving. The appropriate response of a loving God could not be to punish them. They have suffered enough. Surely God should show them the love and grace they never experienced in life? There are many who have suggested and argued that the church needs to abandon this picture of the God of judgment and simply focus on the God of love and grace. It is time to move on.

The problem with moving on from the God of judgment to a God of *only* love and grace can be summed up in one word: Jesus. He did speak about the grace and love of God, but he also said a lot about the judgment of God.[1] One look at the following saying of Jesus (Matt 7:21–23) makes the point clearly enough:

1. Jesus' sayings referring to judgment in the Gospel of Matthew alone include: 4:17; 5:19–22, 29–30, 46; 6:1–2, 4–6, 15–16, 18; 7:1–2, 13–14, 19, 21–23, 24–27; 8:11–12; 10:7,

> Not everyone who says to me "Lord, Lord" will enter into the kingdom of heaven but only the one who does the will of my Father in heaven. 22 Many will say to me on that day "Lord, Lord, did we not prophesy in your name, and cast out demons in your name, and do many works of power in your name?" 23 And then I will swear to you, "I never knew you; depart 'from me, you workers of lawlessness.'"[2]

The day Jesus refers to is the day of judgment, when he will separate the righteous from the unrighteous (Matt 25:31–46). Jesus states that not everybody will enter the kingdom of heaven. Not only that, but he says that some of those who are expecting to do so will not. To make matters worse, they are engaged in Christian ministries—they prophesy, exorcise, and perform miracles *in Jesus' name*. But despite their involvement in Christian ministry, Jesus says he will reject them because in their actions they do not follow God's law.

It makes little sense to pretend that this saying comes from a Jesus who rejected judgment in favor of the love and grace of God. Nor would it be easy to say Jesus is talking about people who have not become Christians. They call Jesus "Lord" and exercise ministries in his name. They are quite convinced they are following him. To some contemporary Christians, Jesus' words here may sound like the worst of Christian teaching, which God sent some of the Protestant reformers to correct with the message "once saved always saved." So, it is interesting to note the following words of John Calvin in his commentary on this passage: "He [Jesus] then exhorts all those who wish to be reckoned among the disciples of Christ, to *withdraw* early *from iniquity*, that Christ may not drive them from his presence, when he shall 'separate the sheep from the goats,' (Matth. xxv. 33.)"[3] It seems that Calvin understands exactly what Jesus is saying and so urges Christians to make a clean break with their past sins and instead live in obedience to God's commands. Jesus' words appear to muddy the waters of any simplistic gospel of love and grace that ignores the judgment of God. Jesus preaches that he will hold all people accountable on that day, including his own.

---

1 5, 23, 26, 28, 32–33, 39, 41–42; 11:21–24; 12:18, 30–32, 36–37, 41–42, 43–45; 13:24–30, 36–43, 47–50; 15:13–14; 16:25–28; 18:3–9, 23–35; 19:16–30; 20:1–16; 21:28–43; 22:1–14; 23:13–15, 33–36; 24:1—25:46; 26:24, 64.

2 Jesus quotes the words "from me, you workers of lawlessness" from Ps 6:9. The Greek of Matthew cites Ps 6:9 LXX *ap emou hoi ergadzomenoi tēn anomian*.

3. Calvin, *Harmony*, 369.

Judgment was a (if not the) keynote of Jesus' ministry, and his sayings on the theme are not easy to downplay. He offers stark and repeated images of the punishment of the unrighteous: "but the sons of the kingdom will be cast out into outer darkness: there, there will be weeping and gnashing of teeth" (Matt 8:12); "and they will cast them into the fiery furnace: there, there will be weeping and gnashing of teeth" (Matt 13:42); "and they will cast them into the fiery furnace: there, there will be weeping and gnashing of teeth" (Matt 13:50). If these statements about the fate of the unrighteous on the day of judgment were not enough, Jesus revisits the theme in parables of judgment, which picture the punishment of the unrighteous: "binding him hand and foot, cast him into outer darkness: there, there will be weeping and gnashing of teeth" (Matt 22:13); "and he will cut him in two and place his portion with the hypocrites: there, there will be weeping and gnashing of teeth" (Matt 24:51); "and cast the worthless slave into outer darkness: there, there will be weeping and gnashing of teeth" (Matt 25:30). The repetition underlines the expectation of judgment that Jesus preached.

Humor has been used to deflect. The apocryphal story tells of a Scottish Presbyterian minister who used to love preaching this stuff. Having warned his flock of the dangers of sin, he was enjoying expounding the texts on the gnashing of teeth in hell. A younger member of his congregation was clearly tired of the theme and, possibly thinking of an elderly relative, piped up, "And minister, what about those who have nae teeth?" The reply was swift and decisive, "Teeth will be provided!"[4] The tale gently mocks the traditional Christian expectation of eternal punishment and so enables the hearer to take it less seriously. The difficulty with such humor is that after the joke is told and (possibly) enjoyed, the awkward sayings of Jesus still remain in the Gospels—as does the question of what we are to do with them.

One possible solution has been provided by some biblical scholars who claim that Jesus never preached about judgment, or at least that it was not a keynote of his ministry. Faced with many questions about the historical reliability of the Gospels, scholars have sought to investigate the texts critically as historians in order to uncover the "real" Jesus. Some have "discovered" a Jesus who was a teacher of Jewish wisdom or social transformation for whom the day of judgment was not a focus of his ministry (basically, by ignoring the many sayings in the Gospels of Matthew, Mark,

---

4. I heard the story from John Ashton (the eminent scholar on the Gospel of John) during one of his lectures at Oxford University in the late 1980s.

Luke, and John in which Jesus does precisely this).[5] The difficulty with this particular solution is that other scholars are equally convinced that Jesus was an apocalyptic preacher whose central vocation was to preach a day of judgment.[6] Those who believe Jesus did preach judgment are more widely followed in the scholarly community. However, the effect of scholarly disagreement (even amongst those who broadly agree on who Jesus was) is that we have no clear and agreed picture of who Jesus was according to critical historical study.[7] So, we are left with the Jesus of the Gospels . . . who preached judgment.

Love wins?

Rob Bell, the author of some popular theology from the United States of America, has offered an alternative vision to the judgment and justice of God as presented by Jesus and the church down the ages. He has written an impassioned and sometimes provocative plea to reconsider the old idea that God will give people eternity to repent and accept his love so everybody has the possibility of being saved in the end—whether they turn to him in this life or the next. He begins by asking a series of seemingly tricky but not necessarily serious questions about the traditional teaching that the gospel must be preached to the ends of the earth so that all may be saved. For example, he asks "what if the missionary gets a flat tire?"[8] None of the questions he asks in his first chapter receive any serious discussion, counter arguments, or counter questions.[9] The point he is making seems to be rhetorical: to get the reader to identify with him in questioning the traditional teaching of the church about heaven, hell, and preaching the gospel (so that

---

5. E.g., For an overview of various scholars who put forward this kind of viewpoint, see Witherington, *Jesus Quest*—especially, pp. 64–92 on John Dominic Crossan, pp. 145–51 on Richard A. Horsley and pp. 163–85 on Elizabeth Schüssler Fiorenza.

6. E.g., Albert Schweitzer, *Quest*; E. P. Sanders, *Jesus*; N. T. Wright, *Victory of God*.

7. E.g., Sanders, Wright, and Casey all agree with Schweitzer that Jesus was an apocalyptic prophet but not on exactly what kind of apocalyptic prophet or exactly what his message was. For example, Wright writes very much as a corrective to Schweitzer on the basis that Schweitzer has misunderstood the nature and meaning of first-century AD Jewish apocalyptic language. For an overview of some of the arguments, see Witherington, *Jesus Quest*, 116–36, 219–32 or Newman, *Restoration of Israel*, 127–41 261–72.

8. Bell, *Love Wins*, 9.

9. Bell, *Love Wins*, 1–19.

The Elephant under the Carpet

as many as respond to Jesus' offer of salvation might be saved on the day of judgment).

Bell then offers a new picture of heaven. He suggests that for Jesus heaven should be understood in terms of what he called "this age" and "the age to come."[10] The age to come has been spoken of by the prophets and is the time when the world will be restored, entirely without suffering.[11] As heaven is the reality of the world without suffering, we ought to live now as we will then and make a difference in the present.[12] Bell then asserts that the Greek word *aiōn* (which we translate as "age" in our Bibles) refers to "a particular *intensity of experience that transcends time*" and so when Jesus talks of the new age he speaks "less about a kind of time that starts when we die, and more about a quality and vitality of life lived now in connection to God."[13] Bell drives home his point that Jesus is really interested in heaven now.[14]

He then turns his attention to hell.[15] He notes that the New Testament talks of a place called *Gehenna* (which we translate as "hell") and that this was a dump outside Jerusalem where garbage was burned.[16] He talks of the living hells of those who suffer injustice.[17] Bell uses the parable of Lazarus and the rich man (Luke 16:19–31) to drive home the point that this story of hell is about the way we live and treat each other in the present.[18] He then surveys many passages in Scripture that speak of God restoring his people to argue that God's purpose is to restore.[19] Tackling Jesus' words on judgment in Matt 25:31–46, he argues that the goats or "those on his left" will not go to eternal suffering but to a period of intense correction (translating the Greek word *aiōn* as "period" and the Greek word *kolasis* as "correction" [Matt 25:46]).[20] So, he suggests that hell after life is corrective and time-

---

10. Bell, *Love Wins*, 30.

11. Bell, *Love Wins*, 31–40.

12. Bell, *Love Wins*, 40–55. He also makes the claims that heaven means God and the place of God's rule, but they are only incidental to his main argument.

13. Bell, *Love Wins*, 56–62, especially 59.

14. It is quite hard to read the rhetorical force of his final paragraphs on this chapter (*Love Wins*, 62) another way.

15. Bell, *Love Wins*, 63–93.

16. Bell, *Love Wins*, 68–69.

17. Bell, *Love Wins*, 70–74.

18. Bell, *Love Wins*, 75.

19. Bell, *Love Wins*, 83–93.

20. Bell, *Love Wins*, 91.

limited and that hell really refers to the suffering caused here and now by not living "in God's world God's way."[21]

On this basis, Bell goes on to affirm the old idea that God will give people the chance to repent throughout all eternity so that in the end everyone will repent, and cites some pretty impressive names in the history of the church to back up his view.[22] He quotes scriptures (e.g., Col 1:20) to back up his argument that Jesus died to bring life to *all*.[23] He argues that Jesus the Word of God is present in all sorts of ways, experiences, and religions bringing salvation.[24] Before ending the book with a story, he argues that the love of God is always greater than the views of mean-minded Christians who believe in judgment largely because they are all washed up by their exhausting experiences of ministry and mission.[25]

Love loses

Rob Bell offers an impassioned plea for his case. However, it simply does not work. His opening chapter uses as much sarcasm as sensible questioning to disrupt the traditional teaching of the church in the readers' minds. The chapter title itself "What about the Flat Tire?" (i.e., people did not hear the gospel because the missionary had a flat tire and so never arrived to preach it) illustrates the point well enough. Given that Bell only asks questions, and offers no discussion in support of even the more sensible questions he asks, he presents no case to answer. However, one very important point needs making by way of response to his questions: God is just and establishes justice. As God is just, his judgment is perfect. Therefore, no Christian believer needs fear that God will act unjustly in any particular scenario—even the ones where they cannot work out what God might do in order to be just. God can act justly regardless of the ability of anyone to imagine what his perfect justice might look like in what seem like hard cases to us.

Bell's argument that heaven is about what happens now does not stand up to scrutiny. In Matthew, Mark, and Luke, nothing in the context of any of Jesus' references to "the age to come" suggests that he is talking about

21. Bell, *Love Wins*, 93.
22. Bell, *Love Wins*, 95–120, especially 107–8.
23. Bell, *Love Wins*, 121–37.
24. Bell, *Love Wins*, 139–61, especially 144–47.
25. Bell, *Love Wins*, 164–91.

anything other than life in the restored earth after judgment day or the punishment that follows the judgment—Jesus uses *aiōn* to refer to both (Matt 12:32; 18:8; 19:16–30; 25:41; 25:46; Mark 10:17–32; Luke 10:25; 18:18–30; 20:35).[26] His references to "this age" all refer to the age before judgment day (Matt 13:39, 40, 49; 24:3; 28:20; Mark 4:19; Luke 16:8; 20:34). In the Gospel of John, eternal life refers to knowing God (e.g., John 17:3) and life after judgment day (e.g., John 6:40). Many sayings about the age in John refer to people having eternal life in the sense that God has granted that they will enter his eternal kingdom on the restored earth after judgment day (e.g., John 12:25). These facts simply do not support Bell's assertion that *aiōn* refers to a particular intensity of experience of God. Words get their meanings from their contexts. The contexts of the word *aiōn* in the Gospels fully support the traditional teaching that there is suffering in this age, and after judgment day there will be a new age in which the sinful will receive just punishment and those who have repented and followed Jesus will live in the restored earth and heavens.

Again, the context of Jesus' use of the word *Gehenna* gives it the meaning it has on his lips. When Jesus speaks of the hell of fire (e.g., Matt 5:22) he uses a contemporary picture of the judgment of God which in one place he fuses with a vision of punishment on God's enemies from Isaiah. Jesus talks of "the hell where their worm never dies and the fire is not extinguished" (Mark 9:47–48), recalling a vision of punishment of God's enemies at the time of the renewal of the heavens and the earth (Isa 66:22–24). Jews at the time of Jesus used the idea of post-mortem punishment in a fiery abyss, which some of them had begun to call *Gehenna* (for the picture of punishment in the fiery abyss, see e.g. 1 En. 90:20-27; for some Jews calling it *Gehenna*, see Sib. Or. 1:100-103).[27] Given this cultural context, Jesus' audience would have heard his words about *Gehenna* to refer to some kind of punishment from which there would be no recovery—let alone an opportunity to progress from it to eternal life.[28]

---

26. E.g., Jesus speaks of "the fire of the age" in Matt 18:8 and 25:41.

27. Nickelsburg, *1 Enoch 1*, 404. 1 Enoch is a Jewish apocalypse written around the time of Jesus. For further details of the work, see the commentary (Nickelsburg, *1 Enoch 1*). For a translation, see Nickelsburg and VanderKam, *1 Enoch*. The Sibylline Oracles is a composite Jewish work written and edited over many years. For an introduction to the work and argument for dating this text as contemporary to Jesus, see the comments of Collins in "Sibylline Oracles," 331–32.

28. Similarly, Collins, *Mark*, 454.

With these points in mind, it becomes more difficult to accept Bell's idea that Jesus talks of a period of correction when he refers to the *kolasin aiōnion* (Matt 25:46). Bell argues that the *kolasis* originally referred to pruning so plants flourish, and so it refers to a specific kind of punishment, "an intense period of correction."[29] The problem for Bell is that all the other references to *kolasis* (or the verb *koladzō*) in the OT, NT, and even the Apocrypha refer to retributive punishment rather than correction (Jer 18:20; Ezek 14:3, 4, 7; 18:30; 43:11; 44:12; Dan 6:13; 2 Macc 4:38; 6:14; 3 Macc 1:3; 3:26; 7:3, 10; 4 Macc 8:9; Wis 3:4; 11:13; 12:15; 14:10; 16:2, 9, 24; 18:11; 19:4; Acts 4:21; 1 John 4:18).[30] The term may be an agricultural word referring to pruning originally, and may have been used by some ancient Greek writers to refer to corrective punishment, but the *biblical* tradition Jesus draws on and continues uses the word to describe *retributive* punishment. All these facts point very firmly in the direction that when Jesus talks of *kolasin aiōnion*, he refers to the punishment of the wicked, not their restoration.

His other arguments can be similarly answered. The list of theologians he uses to support his view is genuine but their views were condemned as heretical in the ninth canon of the Council of Constantinople (AD 543). This view remains heresy. None of the scriptures Bell uses to support his universalist view really do so when read in context. So, for example, immediately after Colossians talks of all things being reconciled to God, it speaks of people being reconciled to God provided they remain steadfast in the faith (Col 1:23)—suggesting that there is the distinct possibility of not being reconciled to God if they do not remain steadfast in faith. There is no avoiding the fact that Jesus spoke of judgment and his sayings are not as easily explained away or avoided as Bell assumes. So, as readers, we have to choose between what Rob Bell thinks a loving God can do and what Jesus thinks the living God will do at the end of time.

A more theological solution?

A different and more intelligent approach to the problem of judgment might be found in reading the judgment sayings of Jesus in the context

---

29. Bell, *Love Wins*, 91.

30. *Kolasis* is a Greek word. The OT was written in Hebrew and Aramaic, and then translated into Greek. Hence, the OT references to *kolasis* given here are of the LXX (or Septuagint), the first translation of the OT into Greek.

of the whole Gospel narrative. In many stories, there are key themes and main plotlines as well as minor themes and subplots. Some things are more important in the story than others. Jesus certainly thought that some things were more important in the Torah (the law and story of God's people in the books of Genesis, Exodus, Leviticus, Numbers, and Deuteronomy) than others.[31] He clearly thought that the implications of God making man and woman (Gen 1:27) and their becoming one flesh (Gen 2:24) was more important than the provision for divorce (Deut 24:1–4), because he said so (Matt 19:4–9). If Jesus thought some aspects of the story of God's people in his Bible were more important than others, then perhaps the same may be true for the Gospel stories. Maybe study of the Gospels could reveal that certain themes are more important than others—possibly that love trumps judgment.

This is the way, for example, that the Swiss New Testament scholar Ulrich Luz reads the Gospel of Matthew.[32] He does not try to deny that this gospel says quite a lot about the coming judgment. In fact, he admits that judgment is a central theme of the Gospel right from the beginning.[33] John the Baptist proclaims the coming judgment (Matt 3:7–12) and so calls people to repent (Matt 3:2, 11). Jesus picks up this call to repent (Matt 4:17). His teaching presupposes that God will judge people (e.g., Matt 7:1), punish them for sin (e.g., Matt 5:22, 29–30; 12:36–37), and reward them for righteousness (e.g., Matt 6:4, 6, 18). He teaches people that he will judge them on this basis on the day of judgment (e.g., Matt 7:21–3; 16:27). He warns those who were expecting to enter the kingdom of heaven on that day but who have no faith in him that they will be left outside (Matt 8:11–12). He instructs his disciples to warn others of the coming judgment (Matt 10:15). He tells whole cities that do not repent of their sin that their judgment will be worse than that of Sodom (Matt 11:20–24). He uses parables to teach the salvation of the righteous and the punishment of the wicked on the day of judgment (e.g., Matt 13:24–30, 36–43, 47–49; 18:23–35; 21:33–41; 22:1–14; 24:45–51; 25:1–30). He warns members of the church not to cause other

---

31. Just in case it needs pointing out, the Torah or law is very much a story with blocks of actual law or commands occupying large chunks of the narrative—but it begins with a story, the creation (Genesis 1), and ends with a story, the death of Moses (Deuteronomy 34), within the wider narrative of the early history of the covenant people from creation up to the point where they were about to enter the promised land.

32. Luz, *Matthew 1–7*; Luz, *Matthew 8–20*; Luz, *Matthew 21–28*. See in particular his helpful discussion of the theme of judgment in Matthew in *Matthew 21–28*, 285–96.

33. Luz, *Matthew 21–28*, 285–86.

disciples to lose their faith as God will judge them for it (Matt 18:6–9). He teaches how difficult it can be for people to enter the kingdom of heaven because they do not want to obey God's commands (Matt 19:24–5). He also teaches of the events leading up to the judgment of God and what will happen at the judgment (Matt 24:1–44; 25:31–46). The thread of judgment runs throughout the teaching ministry of Jesus from his first appearance in the Gospel to his trial and crucifixion.

Luz also admits that Jesus consistently teaches that people will be rewarded or punished for what they have done right or wrong.[34] People will be judged for how they treat others in all of life: from anger and murder (Matt 5:21–22), through sex and adultery (Matt 5:27–30), to careless words (Matt 12:36–37). People will also be rewarded for the righteous actions they do: from faithfully following Jesus (Matt 19:27–30), right down to giving a refreshing drink to one of Jesus' disciples (Matt 10:42). However, Luz finds the prospect of divine judgment that Jesus teaches throughout this gospel to be disturbing:

> . . . an authentic confession of the Lord can only consist of obedience to his commandments. If a person's works are not right, then according to Matthew nothing is right. . . . If that were the case, then the idea of judgment actually could be frightening.[35]

In the Gospel of Matthew, Jesus seems to be teaching that God will judge people *according to what they have done*. For those of us who seek the grace of God in the hope that our sins will be forgiven and not stand against us, Jesus' words do not sound like good news.

So, Luz suggests that reading the Gospel as predominantly about judgment would be a mistake. He claims that Matthew has structured his gospel to prevent us from reading it this way. There may be much material in the Gospel about the day of judgment and all that will happen on that day. However, the Gospel begins and ends with a motif of comfort: the presence of God with us. In the story of Jesus' birth, Matthew says that Jesus was called Emmanuel, which is Hebrew for "God with us" (Matt 1:23). In the last words of the Gospel, Jesus promises to be with his disciples until the end of the age (Matt 28:20). Matthew begins and ends the Gospel with

---

34. Luz, *Matthew 21–28*, 289.
35. Luz, *Matthew 21–28*, 289–90.

this motif because this is the message he wants to leave in the minds of his audience.[36]

> [I]n the Gospel of Matthew, the *story of Jesus*, of the "God with us," takes precedence over ... the *proclamation of Jesus* ... of which the message of judgment is an essential part.

The outline of the story, particularly its beginning and its end, shapes the way we should read the teaching on judgment, which is just part of the story. For Matthew, the presence of God with us is more important than judgment. In other words, mercy triumphs over judgment.

Luz puts it like this. *Either* (a) the Gospel of Matthew presents Jesus as "God with us" *until* the end of time, at which point he becomes the unmerciful judge *or* (b) the God who will judge us is the same person whom we already know as Jesus, "God with us." This Jesus has already made God's love known to us. So, we have nothing to fear from him as judge.[37]

Judgment triumphs after all

The attempt Ulrich Luz makes to soften the theme of judgment in the Gospel of Matthew would be encouraging reading for most people, as few of us relish the prospect of divine judgment. We usually prefer the picture of the God we know showing us love instead. However, Luz' solution does not work. Take another look at the words of Jesus with which we began (Matt 7:21–23):

> Not everyone who says to me "Lord, Lord" will enter into the kingdom of heaven but only the one who does the will of my Father in heaven. 22 Many will say to me on that day "Lord, Lord, did we not prophesy in your name, and cast out demons in your name, and do many works of power in your name?" 23 And then I will swear to you. "I never knew you; depart 'from me, you workers of lawlessness.'"

The people who speak to the Lord Jesus on that day are clearly convinced that they know him. They recognize him and call him "Lord." On their understanding, they ministered in his name. So far as anyone reading the Gospel can tell, they do know him. The problem is not that they do not know him. The problem is that *he* claims not to know *them*. The fact that

---

36. Luz, *Matthew 21–28*, 292.
37. Luz, *Matthew 21–28*, 292.

they knew or thought they knew Jesus seems to be of little use to them in the face of divine judgment. The reason for this is that, so far as Jesus is concerned, their lawless behavior has put them outside his people. They did not live in obedience to his commands, and so their knowledge of the divine judge as Jesus "God with us" does not protect them from the judgment they fear.

Digging deeper into the theme of Jesus "God with us" only opens up further difficulties for the case Luz presents. Matthew announces this theme at the start of his gospel, when an angel tells Joseph to call the son Mary bears Jesus "because he will save his people from their sins" (Matt 1:21). "Jesus" is the Greek version of the Hebrew name "Joshua" (or "Yeshua"), which was popularly thought to be related to the Hebrew word for salvation and the verb "to save."[38] Jesus' name reflects his mission. Matthew then comments (Matt 1:22–23):

> And all of this took place to fulfill the word of the Lord through the prophet Isaiah, "Take note, the virgin will get pregnant and bear a son, and they will give him the name 'Emmanuel,'" which translates as 'God with us.'

Naming the baby boy "Jesus" fulfills this prophecy.[39] The two names, Jesus and Emmanuel, point to the same truth: that Jesus, who is "God with us," will save his people from their sins. The presence of God among his people is not primarily about people knowing God cares because he has come to be with them—it is about his rescuing them from their sins. God with us means God saving us from our sins, and that in turn implies that our sins are serious and we need rescuing from their consequences.[40]

Where Jesus promises his presence at the end of the Gospel, again it has to do with saving people from sin—this time by teaching them to live differently, to obey everything he has commanded. However, his promise is time-limited: "and I will be with you every day *until the end of the age*" (Matt 28:20b). The words sound comforting initially. However, in the Gospel of

---

38. Davies and Allison, *Matthew*, 1:209.

39. The narrative of Matt 1:18–22 fulfills this prophetic word from Isa 7:14. That includes the instruction about naming Jesus and the reason for this. Although Isa 7:14 talks of "Emmanuel" and the angel speaks of "Jesus," the narrator of this story believes these two names point to the same truth. So, France, *Matthew*, 58.

40. Consequences refers here to judgment on that final day, when Jesus comes to judge the living and the dead. There are many other consequences of our sins in terms of our own and others' and creation's suffering. The grace of God covers these too, but not all are sorted out, reconciled, or healed in this world—though some are.

Matthew, Jesus only ever uses these words for the end of the age (Greek *hē synteleia tou aiōnos*) when the judgment of the good and the evil will take place: for example, "so it will be at the end of the age: the Son of Man will send out his angels and they will gather all workers of lawlessness and everything that causes people to stumble in their faith. The angels will cast these into the fiery furnace while the righteous will shine like the sun in the kingdom of their Father" (Matt 13:40–43); and "so it will be at the end of the age: the angels will come and separate the evil from the righteous. They will cast the evil into the fiery furnace" (Matt 13:49–50).[41] In the final words of the Gospel, Jesus promises to be with his disciples until he returns to judge all peoples. We could be forgiven for hearing a note of warning in this promise. These are words of comfort (not least as Jesus promises to be present with his disciples, helping them to teach others to follow him), but they sound a note of judgment too.

It turns out that beginning and ending the Gospel with the presence of God in Jesus does not really perform the function of shielding us from judgment in the way Luz suggests. These "brackets" themselves highlight the theme of judgment and the need for forgiveness. The presence of God in Jesus, Emmanuel "God with us," who saves us from sin, highlights the fact of our sin and the fact that we need saving from it. The presence of God with us until the end of the age does promise salvation from sin in learning to live holy lives but it also underlines the fact that one day we will answer to him as judge.[42] Rather than softening the note of judgment in the Gospel, the theme of "God with us" *heightens* it.

Judgment is a problem that will not go away. Readings of the Gospels like the one we have considered may be ingenious but, ultimately, they fail because the text whispers back to the interpreters that their interpretation ignores the evidence of the text itself. Jesus came to save people from sin but he will also come back to judge all people, including his own. His own words on the topic suggest that he will disown some who call on him but do not follow him. The simple gospel of love and grace needs to hear the words of judgment Jesus speaks and take them seriously. We can try to

---

41. There are two further references to the end of the age in Matthew (Matt 13:39; 24:3), but neither uses the definite article in the original Greek of the New Testament as best we can reconstruct it, (I am using the Greek text of Nestle-Aland 28), although some early witnesses appear to have inserted the definite article in Matt 24:3. It makes no difference to the argument above if these texts are brought into play as they both refer to the day of judgment. See further, Angel, *Inquiring*, 528–29.

42. See further on all this, Angel, *Inquiring*, 527–30.

sweep the elephant under the carpet, but that does not fix the problem. It simply makes the carpet look rather like there is an elephant we are all trying to ignore underneath it. We are probably better off taking a peek under the carpet and getting to know the elephant. Doing this and facing squarely what Jesus really said in the Gospels (including all that he said about judgment) reveals a far greater vision of salvation and of his presence transforming our lives in the here and now than perhaps we ever realized.

3

The Jesus We Don't Want to Know

The problem of judgment will not go away because of Jesus' words on the subject. We cannot simply ignore the judgment of God because we prefer a more amenable gospel of God's love and grace towards us. Jesus preached that there would be a judgment for all humanity, including his own disciples. Shockingly, for some, he taught that he would disown some who were under the impression they were not only his disciples but also ministers of his gospel because they practiced *anomia* or lawlessness (Matt 7:22–23). Jesus wants his disciples not only to hear his words but to *act* on them. After teaching people how to act, live, and pray in the Sermon on the Mount, Jesus tells the following parable (Matt 7:24–27):

> So everyone who hears these words of mine and does them will be like a wise man who built his house on the rock. 25 The rain fell, the rivers swelled, and the winds blew, and they fell on that house, and the house did not fall because its foundation was on the rock. 26 And everyone who hears these words of mine and does not do them will be like a foolish man who built his house on the sand. 27 The rain fell, the rivers swelled, and the winds blew, and they beat that house and it fell. It completely collapsed.

Both the wise and the foolish hear Jesus' words. Both are aware of his teaching. The difference between the wise and the foolish is not that the wise know about Jesus and the foolish do not. They both know about Jesus and have heard his commands. The difference is this: the wise live out his teaching and obey his commands. The foolish do not. Jesus solves the problem of lawlessness by teaching people how to live and, in this parable, he states that their response to his teaching determines how they will fare on the day of judgment.

Jesus sees his task as teaching but not in the manner of the modern Western educator. Jesus does not teach his disciples so that they *understand*. Jesus teaches his disciples so that they *obey*. Discipleship is not about learning *ideas*, being able to critically assess them, and then maybe adopt them. Discipleship happens when those who have heard Jesus' words change the way they live and act according to his teaching and commands. This is the point of the Parable of the Wise and Foolish Builders, and it tells us something critical, both about the kind of teacher Jesus is and about the kind of lives Jesus calls us to live as his disciples.

This may throw down a further challenge to the way some people understand the basic teachings of the Christian faith. With good reason they emphasize the fact that we cannot earn our way into the kingdom of God at the end of time, because we all sin. We all fall foul of at least some of God's commands and are deserving of punishment for our wrongdoings. Quite properly, they teach that Christ died on our behalf that we might be forgiven our sins. Then they add that nothing can separate us from the love of God, as Paul wrote (Rom 8:38–39). They then generally forget to note that later in the same letter Paul warned his readers: "so take note of the generosity and severity of God: severity upon those who have fallen, but the generosity of God towards you personally, provided you continue in his generosity, or you too will be cut off" (Rom 11:22). And again, in the same letter he warns them against bullying behavior towards other Christians on the basis that "we will all stand before the judgment seat of God" (Rom 14:10). For Paul, at least, the work of salvation does not stop with our accepting God's forgiveness of our sins. He seems to be on the same page as Jesus: lives must be changed to live out Christ's teachings. Jesus Christ did win the victory over sin and death on the cross, but if we as his followers take this at all seriously, we do not rest on *his* laurels—we pick up and carry *our* crosses. We become his disciples and live out his teachings. (Just in case anyone might misunderstand me, I am emphatically not saying we are saved by our good behavior. We are saved from sin by Christ's work on the cross, where he took the punishment for our sin. However, his work does not stop there. He wants to save us from sin in the present by teaching us his ways also.)

Jesus came to die for our sins, *but he also came to teach us the way to live.* The Gospel presents Jesus as a rabbi, a teacher who explained how people might *obey* God in all areas of their lives so that they might truly love him with their whole heart, soul, body, and mind. Most of Jesus' earthly ministry was taken up with teaching people how to live to serve God in this way, in obedience to his commands. Jesus taught people how to obey God as he wanted them to have eternal life with him, just as in the Parable of the Wise and Foolish Builder. The Gospel presents Jesus' ministry as the teacher of the way to life in some detail. Exploring this detail (as we will below) can bring surprises. But it helps us to begin to understand how Jesus saw his teaching ministry as the answer to the problem of judgment.

An apocalyptic teacher

Jesus came to die for our sins, but he also came to teach us the way to life. The end-goal of Jesus' teaching ministry is to bring people into the community of God's people who will live forever with him in the kingdom of heaven. Jesus begins this ministry proclaiming the words "repent for the kingdom of heaven has drawn near" (Matt 4:17). What Jesus means by "the kingdom of heaven has drawn near" is that God is about to come and judge, and that people will be judged according to their righteousness. If they have obeyed God's commands they will be rewarded with everlasting life. If they have not, they will be punished according to their sins and forfeit everlasting life.[1] Assuming that people are sinners, Jesus instructs them to repent so

---

1. I realize that for many the kingdom of heaven (or kingdom of God) means "the action of God," "God's rule in the world," "heaven," "God working miracles amongst us by his Spirit," "the radical political transformation of society," or something like one or more of these things. However, these definitions will not do, not least because they make no sense of Jesus' parables where he compares the kingdom to things that involve separating people and ultimately casting some of them into outer darkness (i.e. the Parable of the Weeds of the Field [Matt 13:24–30, 36–43]; the Parable of the Net [Matt 13:47–50], which cannot refer to anything except the final judgment). Going back to the psalms about God as king in the Old Testament (e.g., Psalms 96, 97, and 99), the kingdom of God starts with the judgment of God. He rewards the righteous, punishes the wicked, and establishes justice and peace in Israel and throughout the world. This is the action of God. It is how he will establish his rule, his justice, and his peace. It is how he will bring healing and restoration to people, society, and the whole of creation. When we understand this to be the meaning of the kingdom of God, every saying of Jesus about

that they may be forgiven their sin and that it will not stand against them on the day of judgment. However, repentance does not simply involve asking forgiveness. Literally, repentance means "turning your mind around." So, Jesus expects people who repent not simply to ask forgiveness of their sins but to live renewed and good lives, following his commands.[2]

Repentance leads to morally good behavior. If someone turns their mind and heart around, they decide to turn away from the wrongs they have been doing. This is the appropriate response to recognizing that certain thoughts, ways of speaking, or actions are sinful. It makes little sense to apologize for thinking, saying, and doing such things only to carry on doing them. That kind of "saying sorry" is not what Jesus means by repentance. That sort of behavior involves turning our minds around momentarily and then turning them straight back again. True repentance involves apologizing sincerely for past sins and turning our lives around morally so that we are committed to living according to the commandments of God.

When Jesus called people to repent because the kingdom of heaven had drawn near, he was not expecting them to say sorry and then hang around waiting for their time to come when they would go to be with God—or for the time that God would come again. He called them to repentance, healed them, and taught them (Matt 4:23).

> And he was going around the whole of Galilee teaching in their synagogues and preaching the good news of the kingdom of heaven and healing every disease and every ailment among the people.

Jesus taught the people he was calling to repentance. He taught them how to obey God. Many of his teachings explain how those who follow him are to obey God's commandments in the law that God had given Moses. Jesus was not a moral teacher of a wonderful new love ethic. He was an interpreter of God's commandments in the law, the Torah. In this, Jesus was what every rabbi at the time sought to be. Jesus taught people how to obey God's commands because repentance involves asking forgiveness for sins *and* changing our ways so that we obey God.

---

the kingdom of God makes sense. Some of us need to kiss goodbye to our notions of the kingdom of God and reclaim the kingdom Jesus taught. On this, I would like to write more in another book on another occasion.

2. As in the Gospel of John, which presents Jesus saying to the woman caught in adultery: "go, and from now on sin no longer" (John 8:11). I am more than aware of the textual questions around the authenticity of this text, for which see Barrett (*St John*, 598–92) and Carson (*John*, 333).

Jesus did this because he wanted as many as would respond to his preaching and teaching to enter the kingdom of heaven on judgment day. He seems to have accepted that not all would respond. This much is clear in the Parable of the Wise and Foolish Builders (Matt 7:24–27), which he told precisely because he could envisage the situation where people heard his teaching and did nothing about it. Jesus is an apocalyptic teacher who instructs people how to live out his commands so as to prepare them for the day of judgment. Jesus teaches repentant sinners how to obey God's law so that they might be judged forgiven *and* righteous on that day.

A teacher like Moses

The fact that Jesus was an interpreter of the Torah, or law, may still strike some people as odd. One of the strange myths that permeates some church communities is that Jesus came to do away with the Torah and replace it with something entirely different. Most versions of this strange myth suggest that Jesus came to replace the law with love. This is untrue. Jesus drew both of his great love commands (love God and love your neighbor) from the Torah, and it makes little sense to say that Jesus replaced the commands of the law with commands from the law. Jesus was an *interpreter* of God's commandments in the law, teaching people how to follow them so that they could live the kind of lives of obedience and love to which God calls all those who repent of their sins. The way the Gospels tell the story of Jesus underlines this point. The Gospel writers, especially Matthew, make a point of comparing Jesus with Moses to underline the fact that Jesus had come to interpret the law and so teach people how to live out God's commandments.

Moses was the great servant of God who led Israel out of Egypt. With his brother Aaron as his mouthpiece, he stood up to Pharaoh and demanded that he free the Hebrew slaves so that they could go and worship their God in the wilderness (e.g., Exod 10:3). After the plagues God sent on Egypt when Pharaoh refused to let his people go, Moses led the Hebrews out of Egypt. Despite many years in the desert, Moses led them to the edge of the promised land (Deut 34:1–4). During this journey from Egypt to the promised land, particularly at Mount Sinai (Exod 20:1—31:18) and on the plain opposite Suph (Deut 1:1—30:20), Moses gave Israel the Torah—which included the commandments of God that taught them how to live as his people.

The Jesus You *Really* Didn't Know

The Gospel stories compare Jesus to Moses in many ways. One example of the many comparisons made between Jesus and Moses may be found in the story of Jesus' birth in the Gospel of Matthew.[3] Herod ordered all the children aged two and under in Bethlehem and the surrounding area to be killed (Matt 2:16) just as Pharaoh ordered all the Hebrew male babies to be killed (Exod 1:15–16). Mary and Joseph flee Herod's attempt to kill Jesus (Matt 2:13–14) just as Moses flees Pharaoh's attempt to kill him (Exod 2:15). After the death of Herod, Joseph is commanded to return to his homeland (Matt 2:19–20) just as Moses was commanded to return to Egypt after the death of Pharaoh (Exod 4:19).[4] This example of similarities between Jesus and Moses in the story of Jesus' birth makes the point that Matthew compares Jesus to Moses. There are many other points of comparison of Jesus and Moses in the Gospels, all of which underline the fact that Gospels want us to understand that Jesus is somehow like Moses.[5]

The main way in which Jesus is like Moses is that he taught the true interpretation of the law, just as Moses first gave the law. At the time of Jesus, Moses had become known in Jewish tradition as the great lawgiver for his part in giving Israel the laws that God commanded his people to keep. By this time, some Old Testament books had already called the Torah "the Law of Moses" (Ezra 3:2; 7:6; Neh 8:1; 13:1) because Moses was the person through whom God gave Israel his commandments (Neh 1:7–9; 8:14; 9:14; 10:29).[6] The Jewish historian Josephus tells us that five books were

---

3. The comparisons are not limited to Matthew and Exodus. Matthew also seems to be comparing Jesus with Moses in contemporary retellings of the Exodus story. Concerned that Mary was pregnant before their marriage, Joseph was contemplating separation from her and an angel told him to take her in marriage (Matt 1:18–21). In the retelling of the story of Moses by the Jewish historian Josephus (first century AD), Moses' father Amram was worried about his wife's pregnancy and God appeared to him in a dream to comfort him (*Ant.* 2:210–16). Just as Joseph is told that Jesus will save his people from their sins (Matt 1:21), so Josephus wrote that Amram was told that Moses would deliver the Hebrews from Egypt (*Ant.* 2:15–16). Just as Herod gave this instruction because he had heard that another king had been born (Matt 2:1–8), so Josephus wrote that Pharaoh commanded the killing of the Hebrew babies because of a prophecy that one of them would exalt Israel over Egypt (*Ant.* 2:205–7).

4. For these comparisons and those in Josephus, see Davies and Allison, *Matthew*, 1:192–93. For the remarkable verbal parallels in the Greek text of Matt 2:19–20 and Exod 4:19 LXX, see Davies and Allison, *Matthew*, 1:271.

5. See Allison, *New Moses*.

6. I am assuming a fifth or fourth century BC date for the writing of Ezra and Nehemiah, see Williamson, *Ezra, Nehemiah*, xxxv–xxxvi. A later date would not affect the argument here, which simply assumes that the Ezra and Nehemiah were written prior

associated with Moses: "and five of these are the books of Moses which contain the laws and the community history from the origin of humanity to his [Moses'] death" (*Ag. Ap.* 1:39). The five books which contain these laws and tell this story ending at the death of Moses are Genesis, Exodus, Leviticus, Numbers, and Deuteronomy. This fivefold pattern of the "Law of Moses" had become so special that some contemporary Jews who wrote and ordered other Jewish religious texts, such as the Psalms and *1 Enoch*, imitated it.[7]

Matthew also imitated it by ordering Jesus' teaching into five blocks in his gospel. A simple comparison with Mark or Luke shows this up clearly. All follow a similar storyline. After Jesus' baptism, he heals and teaches in Galilee. Then he travels to Jerusalem. Around this time, he is transfigured. When he arrives in Jerusalem, there are clashes that lead to his crucifixion. He rises from the dead.[8] Matthew, Mark, and Luke all develop this shared basic storyline in different ways, but only Matthew inserts five blocks of teaching in his narrative. These blocks of teaching are: the Sermon on the Mount, which outlines righteous living (Matt 5:1—7:27); instruction on how the disciples should preach the good news throughout Israel (Matt 10:5–42); the parables of the kingdom (Matt 13:1–52); teaching on living as a community of disciples, particularly teaching about humility and forgiveness (Matt 18:1–35); and finally, teaching about judgment (Matt 24:1—25:46). Each of these blocks of teaching ends with a very similar phrase: "and it happened when Jesus finished these words" (Matt 7:28); "and it happened when Jesus finished instructing his twelve disciples" (Matt 11:1); "and it happened when Jesus finished these parables" (Matt 13:53); "and it happened when Jesus finished these words" (Matt 19:1); and finally, "and it happened when Jesus finished all these words" (Matt 26:1). The use of the repeated phrase "and it happened when Jesus finished" after each block of teaching and nowhere else in the Gospel underlines the fact that Matthew wants his audience to understand that these five blocks of teaching are to be linked together.[9] That the final one reads "finished *all* these words" (Matt

---

to Jesus.

7. Gundry, *Matthew*, 10–11.

8. There are various endings to the Gospel of Mark in early manuscripts. Most scholars today argue that Mark ended at Mark 16:8 (Collins, *Mark*, 797–801). If this is so, then there is no resurrection narrative in this gospel. However, the angel announces to the women that Jesus has risen (Mark 16:6). So even if there is no resurrection narrative as such, the resurrection remains part of the story of Mark.

9. The various English translations render these words differently. My translation

26:1) simply stresses that the blocks of teaching end there. The fact that Matthew orders Jesus' teaching into five blocks like the five books of the Torah suggests that Matthew compares Jesus' teaching to the law given by Moses.[10] That the phrase by which Matthew signals this ("and it happened when Jesus finished all these words") is reminiscent of a phrase used in the Torah to indicate that Moses had finished giving his teaching ("and Moses finished speaking all these words" [Deut 31:1]) underlines the point.[11] Matthew even places Jesus on a mountain for the first block of teaching, just as Moses receives the law on Mount Sinai.[12] Matthew portrays Jesus as a teacher and lawgiver like Moses, the great lawgiver.

Moses did not teach God's commands simply so that Israel might be good but so that they could experience prosperity, freedom, and blessing in the promised land. This is clear from Moses' instruction to teach God's commandments to each new generation (Deut 11:18–21).

> You shall put these words of mine in your heart and soul, and you shall bind them as a sign on your hand and fix them as an emblem on your forehead. 19 Teach them to your children, talking about them when you are at home and when you are away, when you lie down and when you rise. 20 Write them on the doorposts of your house and on your gates, 21 *so that your days and the days of your children may be multiplied in the land that the* LORD *swore to your ancestors to give them, as long as the heavens are above the earth.*

God had not rescued his people from slavery so that they could live as sinfully as their Egyptian overlords (e.g., Deut 5:12–15). God rescued his people from slavery and gave them the law so that they could live in justice and peace. If Israel obeyed the law they would experience God's blessing in

---

"and it happened when Jesus finished" is a literal (and slightly clumsy) rendering of the Greek *kai egeneto hote etelesen ho Iēsous*.

10. Scholars differ over whether this is a new Torah, a replacement for the Torah, or a final interpretation of the Torah. A classic statement of this thesis may be found in Bacon, *Studies in Matthew*. The thesis did not originate with him as he notes he follows an interpretation that in critical scholarship is half a century old (*Studies in Matthew*, xiv) and that he argues was already known in the early centuries of the church (*Studies in Matthew*, xvi).

11. Hays, *Echoes*, 144. The Greek is not identical, but similar enough to warrant Hays' suggestion that the Matthean phrase (*kai egeneto hote etelesen ho Iēsous pantas tous logous*) echoes that in Deuteronomy (*kai synetelesen Mōusēs lalōn pantas tous logous*).

12. The point is commonplace, not least as Luke places a similarly large sermon with much of the same material on the plain (Luke 6:17–49). See, for example, Davies and Allison, *Matthew*, 1:423–24.

the land, and that if they did not God would punish them by taking them away from the land into captivity again (e.g., Deut 28:1—29:1).

Like Moses, Jesus teaches people not simply so that they are good but so that they will experience God's blessing.[13] This is clear from Jesus' teaching itself. The Parable of the Wise and Foolish Builders makes it clear that those who hear his words and put them into practice experience blessing, whereas those who do not put them into practice do not (Matt 7:24-27). Elsewhere, Jesus teaches that on the day of judgment, the angels will gather up all those who live lawlessly and cast them into the fiery furnace (Matt 13:41-42). On that day the Son of Man will reward those who fed the hungry, gave the thirsty a drink, welcomed the stranger, clothed the naked, took care of the sick, and visited those in prison (Matt 25:34-40). Jesus preaches repentance so that people are forgiven by God and may enjoy eternal life with him. However, repentance involves turning back to God and so committing to live in obedience to him. Jesus teaches that the solution to the problem of *anomia*, or lawlessness, is repentance—and that means asking for forgiveness for sins, and living in renewed relationship with God, which leads to changing our ways and living in obedience to God.

The only teacher

Jesus may be like the great lawgiver Moses, but he is also more than Moses. Not only is Jesus not like a modern Western educator, in one rather stark way he was not like the rabbis of his day either. Around the time of Jesus, there was a tradition that Moses had handed the Torah down in an unbroken chain to the rabbis (m. 'Abot 1:1—2:8).[14] Moses received the Torah on Sinai, handed it on to Joshua, who handed it onto the elders, who handed it on to the prophets, who handed it on to the men of the great assembly (m. 'Abot 1:1) before it was later handed on to rabbis Hillel and Shammai

---

13. Blessing with Jesus looks a little different to simply life in the land God promised, health, and prosperity. Blessing involves these things, as Jesus promises that anyone who has given up material blessings in this life will inherit one hundred times as much, and eternal life, when he comes again to judge the nations (Matt 19:27-30). Mark records a saying in which Jesus says they will receive such blessings both in this age and in eternal life (Mark 10:28-31). But Jesus also says we are blessed when people revile and persecute us because we will receive a great reward in heaven when he comes to judge (Matt 5:11-12), which suggests that we are to see our blessing in suffering too.

14. Rabbis were (and are) teachers of the Torah.

(m. 'Abot 1:12).[15] According to this tradition, the men of the great assembly said three things: "be prudent in judgment, raise up many disciples, make a fence for the Torah" (m. 'Abot 1:1). In order to do these things, the rabbis would discuss and teach the Torah. As they interpreted the Torah, they would hand down their tradition of interpretation to their disciples. The Mishnah (the earliest document we possess that brings together the teachings of the early rabbis, compiled around AD 200) catalogues these interpretations of the Torah.[16] The tradition of interpretation offered not simply the law but also the interpretations of the law that the many authorized voices (deemed to give a sound interpretation of the law) offered. This process was ongoing, as further interpretation was offered by each new generation of rabbis.

The traditions about Jesus are very different. The Gospels contain the voice of only one authoritative rabbi: Jesus.[17] In the Gospel narratives, the Pharisees and scribes *ask questions*, but only Jesus *gives the answers* (e.g., Matt 19:3–9; 22:34–40).[18] Not only do the Gospel writers ensure that we only hear Jesus' voice as authoritative but they also suggest that other voices are without authority: "and the crowds were astounded at his [Jesus'] teaching because he was teaching them as someone who had authority and not like their scribes" (Matt 7:28–29).[19] The Gospel presents Jesus as the only authoritative interpreter of the Torah.

In some ways, this was remarkable. Teaching was right at the heart of the life and faith of the covenant people. The Torah instructed parents to teach their children God's commandments. Both the law and later Jewish traditions instructed that priests were to teach the Torah to the nation (Deut 31:9–13; Neh 8:1–18; Sir 45:6–7, 17), and at the time of Jesus the priests were still the official teachers of the law.[20] At least one contemporary

---

15. The great assembly was an assembly of 120 scribes, wise people, and prophets in the period between the last of the Old Testament prophets and the time of Jesus.

16. For a translation of the Mishnah, see Jacob Neusner, *Mishnah*. Neusner (*Mishnah*, xvi) dates the compilation and editing of the Mishnah around AD 200.

17. This point is put forward and fully explored by Samuel Byrskog, *Only Teacher*.

18. Even the scribe in the Gospel of Mark who offers an authoritative affirmation of Jesus' answer to his question about the greatest commandment, receives a response from Jesus that, although affirming, demonstrates very clearly who really has the authority to interpret the Torah (Mark 12:28–34). When the scribe commends Jesus for his sound teaching, Jesus responds "you are not far from the kingdom of God" (Mark 12:34).

19. Similarly, Mark 1:22.

20. Sanders, "Law," 261.

Jewish philosopher, Philo of Alexandria, pictured the ancient kings of Israel as great students and teachers of the law. Philo claims that the kings of Israel would copy out the whole of the Torah themselves, and by doing this they found that the law imprinted itself on their souls. This enabled them both to live by it and to rule the nation according to its commandments in justice and equality (*Spec. Laws* 4:160-67).[21] Although this might be an idealized picture of these kings (some of whom manifestly did not follow the law [e.g., Manasseh, 2 Kgs 21:1-18]), it demonstrates the ideal that at least some Jews around the time of Jesus held: that the Torah should be at the heart of the life of God's people. The teaching of the law and obedience to its commands was supposed to lie right at the heart of the life of the nation, and the priests were to teach it to the people.

Therefore, suggesting that only one person had the authority to interpret the Torah seems to go right against most of the culture—particularly when that person does not seem to have been recognized by the official priesthood as a priest. However, it was not entirely without precedent. There was one renewal movement in Palestine that had grown up in the two centuries before Jesus was born, the Essenes, whose main base was at Qumran and who were responsible for writing and collating the Dead Sea Scrolls. This community galvanized around a figure they called the Teacher of Righteousness (CD 1:9-11) and they held that he alone taught the true way of God (CD 20:1, 32).[22] So Jesus and his followers were not the only Jewish movement to suggest that only one person was the true teacher of the ways of God. Similarly, there is no reason to suppose that all the Pharisees were priests and yet many at the time saw their rabbis as authoritative teachers.[23] So Jesus and his followers were not the only movement in the Judaism of his time that accepted as authoritative the teaching of people

---

21. Philo of Alexandria (50 BC to AD 50) was a Jewish philosopher living and working in Egypt and contemporary of Jesus. His vision of the king of Israel as a student and teacher of the Torah expounds the instructions for the king found in Deut 17:14-20.

22. On the Teacher of Righteousness, see Murphy-O'Connor, "Teacher of Righteousness," 340-41.

23. For this point, see Saldarini, "Pharisees," 289-303. For evidence that many contemporary Jews followed the teaching of the rabbis, or Pharisees, see Josephus, *War* 2:162; *Ant.* 13:298; 18:15. The rabbinic movement is generally understood to have started with the Pharisees. However, it ought to be noted that there is some debate amongst scholars about exactly who the Pharisees were, what they practiced, and why. For a nice overview of the debate with a good introduction to the Pharisees, see Meier, *Marginal Jew*, 3:311-40. For a strong case that the Pharisees were more than just a holiness cult but had a political agenda, see Wright, *People of God*, 181-203.

who were not priests. Even so, at least the Pharisees were a community of interpretation in which there were a number of authoritative interpreters of the Torah, namely their rabbis. By stark contrast, the early Christians believed that Jesus was the *only* true teacher of the law.

Matthew traces this viewpoint back to Jesus himself. He records Jesus as saying the following words to his disciples and the wider public (Matt 23:8–10).

> You are not to be called "rabbi" because you have one teacher and you are all disciples. 9 And do not call anyone your father on earth, as you have only one father—the heavenly one. 10 Nor are you to be called instructors because you have one instructor, the Messiah.[24]

Jesus clearly identifies rabbis as teachers and instructs his disciples not to accept anyone calling them rabbi.[25] In making this instruction, he breaks the chain of interpretation that, according to contemporary Jewish tradition, stretched from Moses down to the rabbis of the Pharisaic movement of his day. Jesus' disciples were not to understand themselves as rabbis in training who would one day become the authoritative interpreters of the Torah. They were to accept that there was now one true and final interpreter of the Torah, their own rabbi Jesus.[26] Having made the point, Jesus goes on to underline it. They are all brothers in a learning community and they have only one Father, their heavenly Father.[27] They are not to be called instructors, or teachers in the faith, as they have only one teacher in the faith—namely the Messiah Jesus.

So, Jesus was and is a certain sort of teacher—for want of a better description, an *apocalyptic* teacher. He teaches his disciples how to obey

24. I translate the Greek word *adelphoi* (Matt 23:8) as "disciples" rather than the more literal "brothers" or "brothers and sisters." This is the meaning of the word here (Davies and Allison, *Matthew*, 3:276). Already in the Gospel, Jesus has identified his true brothers and sisters as those who do the will of his Father in heaven (Matt 12:46–50).

25. Davies and Allison (*Matthew*, 3:275), although they suggest that the title "rabbi" became a technical term for a teacher late in the first century AD and so this saying does not go back to Jesus. For evidence from Jewish sources that the title "rabbi" was already used of Jewish teachers in the first century, see Luz, *Matthew 21-28*, 105–6, especially n.80. See also Nolland, *Matthew*, 926–27. The evidence of the Gospels themselves suggests that the title rabbi was used for teachers, not simply here in Matt 23:8, but elsewhere, e.g., John 1:38.

26. Similarly, France, *Matthew*, 183, 863.

27. For "father" as a term used of a rabbi or teacher, see Luz, *Matthew 21-28*, 105 n.81.

God's commandments in the belief and knowledge that one day he will come again to judge the living and the dead. On that day, he will reward everyone according to what they have done: those who have done good will reap their reward, and those who have done evil their punishment. In the light of this, Jesus proclaims that people need to repent of their sins, turn around and learn to live righteous and godly lives. Having received forgiveness of our sins, we are in renewed relationship with God, which means that we must learn to live in obedience to all that Jesus commands (because God calls his people to live according to his commands so that they live in justice and peace rather than sin). Accepting forgiveness and so following Jesus brings eternal life. Just as Moses taught God's law to people who had been rescued from slavery, Jesus teaches God's commands to those who have been rescued from the slavery of sin. However, we are not bound to obey the law of Moses *as the Pharisees were teaching it*, but we are to live in obedience to God's commands *as Jesus taught them*, because he is the final interpreter of the law.

Jesus and the Pharisees

Setting himself up as the one true teacher of the law inevitably brought Jesus into conflict with other rabbis, who saw their own interpretations of the Torah as faithful and valid. Studying this conflict will tell us more about the kind of teacher Jesus was and is, and in turn will help us to understand better the problem of the judgment we face and what we are expected to do to prepare for it. However, studying this conflict will also bring us face to face with certain stereotypes of the Pharisees and Jesus' disagreements with them that simply do not stand up to scrutiny. There are some comforting myths that have gone around (and still do go around) many churches, which compare Jesus and the Pharisees in ways that help some Christians feel better about themselves and relax into an easy faith that does not demand too much of them. These comforting myths have been challenged by historians, and they do not really stand up to a careful reading of the biblical text. They need stripping away to see what is really going on and to understand the differences between Jesus and the Pharisees. Some of these differences are very different from the comforting myths many of us have told ourselves.

Perhaps it would be helpful to begin by rehearsing the outlines of the comforting myths I have in mind. The following words of the popular evangelical author from the United States of America, Philip Yancey, express the popular myth very well:

> Jesus came to earth "full of grace and truth," says the gospel of John, and that phrase makes a good summary of his message. First, grace: in contrast to those who tried to complicate the faith and petrify it with legalism, Jesus preached a simple message of God's love. For no reason—certainly not because we deserve it—God has decided to extend to us his love that comes free of charge, no strings attached, "on the house."[28]

According to these popular comforting myths, the Pharisees were *legalists*. In practice, this means that they were obsessed with obedience to the law—not only the law itself, but also their own interpretations of it. The Pharisees had added many, basically pointless, commands to those already in the law. The law was too much of a burden for people and they were incapable of obeying it. With the commands of the Pharisees added in, pleasing God was impossible. The Pharisees were also moral hypocrites who not only added laws upon laws but they did not even obey these laws themselves. Without any humanity or compassion, they demanded obedience to all God had commanded and to all they had added. By contrast, Jesus taught love. He showed people that God loved them as his very own children. God wanted people to understand his love and not be lost in legalism. Moreover, Jesus taught that love replaced commandments. God only wanted people to do the loving thing. As a result, Jesus set an example of breaking the rules in order that the loving thing may be done instead—and he taught his followers to do the same. So, none of Jesus' followers are under obligation to meet moral demands that are too much for them. Instead, we are to seek an ever-deepening knowledge of God's love for us. God only calls us to do what is loving and anyone who demands too much from us is a legalist.

This comforting myth is simply not true. Nor is it fair on the Pharisees, some of whom seem (at least to me) far closer in their spirituality to many of their Christian detractors than these detractors might care to admit. The truth is rather different and deserves a closer look—not least because it goes a long way to uncovering what kind of teacher Jesus actually was and what he really taught his disciples. He may turn out to look rather more like a Pharisee in some ways than we thought and this may make some of us feel

---

28. Yancey, *Jesus*, 95. I quote Yancey simply because these words sum up the popular myth so well. There is much in this book I find really helpful and not quite as simplistic as the lines I cite here.

uncomfortable. However, it is better to look under the carpet and see what lies beneath than to live in denial of the truth.

Breaking the law

Chief amongst the comforting myths is that Jesus broke the law for the sake of love and to teach others to break the law when that is "the loving thing to do." The following words of Jesus on obedience to God's commands make this very difficult to believe (Matt 5:17–20):

> Do not say to yourselves that I have come to destroy the law or the prophets: I have not come to destroy them but to fulfill them. 18 Honestly, I tell you, until heaven and earth pass away not one of the tiniest bits of punctuation will drop off the page of the law, until all things are accomplished. 19 Therefore, whoever loosens up one of the least of these commands and teaches other people to do the same will be called least in the kingdom of heaven. Whoever does them and teaches them, these people will be called great in the kingdom of heaven. 20 Honestly, I tell you that unless your righteousness more than exceeds that of the scribes and the Pharisees, you will not enter the kingdom of heaven.[29]

These words make it very difficult to claim that Jesus was not interested in people obeying God's commands. On a plain reading, they seem to suggest that Jesus says that the whole law of God remains in place until heaven and earth pass away and that anybody who fails to teach the law in its entirety will diminish their reputation for eternity—although they will experience eternal life with God. Nonetheless, they will only experience that if their obedience to God's commands exceeds that of the scribes and Pharisees. The bar seems to be set quite high.

Many suggestions have been made for softening the effect of these words. One very popular suggestion is that these are the words of the gospel writer, Matthew, rather than the words of Jesus. After all, they are only found in the Gospel of Matthew. So perhaps he made them up, or found them in an early tradition that came from another first-century AD Christian, and

---

29. I admit to translating the Greek words *iōta hen ē mia keraia* in v. 18 somewhat freely. "One iota or tiny diacritical mark" does not lend itself to being easily understood. An iota is a tiny letter in the Greek alphabet and the exact reference of the *keraia* (literally "little horn"), although not agreed by scholars, is often understood to be some tiny mark in Hebrew or Aramaic writing—see Davies and Allison, *Matthew*, 1:491.

edited them into his gospel text.[30] While this is possible, it is not certain and it does not solve the problem. The many conflicting arguments about who the historical Jesus was and how many of the words ascribed to him in the Gospels he actually said continue to rumble on without any sign of their being resolved to everyone's satisfaction.[31] Until they are, no one view on which words in the Gospels really come from Jesus can claim to be true. For understanding Jesus, this leaves us with two basic options: either accept the views of one scholarly viewpoint over the others or accept the words of the biblical texts as they stand as the best insights into Jesus we have and can have. Regardless of which option we choose, the fact remains that the universal church down the centuries has accepted the words of Jesus *found in the four New Testament Gospels* as authoritative—and not any one particular biblical scholar's reconstruction of Jesus' teaching.[32]

Another suggestion is that Jesus has fulfilled the law and the prophets. The Torah only held authority for a certain period of time. When Jesus the Messiah came, the Torah was no longer binding in the same way but was subordinate to the authoritative teaching of Jesus. Given the way in which Matthew presents Jesus as the final interpreter of the law, there has to be something in this idea. Jesus' teaching fulfills and completes the law. Jesus speaks of his teaching as "my yoke" (Matt 11:29). The yoke was a rabbinic metaphor for the law. No other rabbi ever spoke of *their* yoke. There was

---

30. For example, Luz (*Matthew 1–7*, 221) argues that Matthew appropriates a Jewish Christian tradition here.

31. The story of the quest or quests for the historical Jesus up to 1988 are described in Neill and Wright, *Interpretation*. Since then, there have been many more historical Jesus works, for example: Meyer, *Aims*; Sanders, *Jesus*; Allison, *Jesus of Nazareth*. Probably the greatest of these projects are the ongoing work of John Paul Meier (*A Marginal Jew*—five volumes, to date) and N. T. Wright (Christian Origins and the Question of God—four volumes, to date).

32. I do not doubt that some professional biblical scholars would balk at this response to their individual quests for the historical Jesus. However, it remains true. I too wish that my own small contribution to the quest for understanding the historical Jesus were universally acknowledged as true—but it is not. We simply have to accept the state of play until the day we all agree. Much the same is true of attempts to "recover" the "real" Jesus from early traditions that have parallels in gnostic "gospels," such as the Gospel of Thomas or the Gospel of Peter. No one of these attempts commands universal agreement amongst scholars. What is more, I am unaware of any orthodox Christian church that has formally refused to accept the canonical authority of the Gospels of Matthew, Mark, Luke, and John or which has formally accepted the authority of any other ancient text purporting to be a gospel.

only the yoke of the law.[33] Jesus speaks of his interpretation of the law as if it is the law—because for him it is the law.

Pointing this out raises the question of what Jesus expected his followers to do with the commandments that he did not teach. The New Testament scholar Dick France has argued that all things were accomplished (Matt 5:19) when Jesus was born on earth. This means that parts of the law were laid aside during his earthly life.[34] However, his argument does not sit easily with the statement in v. 19 that those who loosen up the binding nature of "one of the least of these commandments" shall bring dishonor on themselves in the kingdom of heaven and the statement in v. 18 that the commandments are binding until heaven and earth pass away.[35] If this refers to heaven and earth literally passing away, this clearly has not happened.[36] Moreover, there is nothing in the Gospel of Matthew that suggests that heaven and earth passed away figuratively when Jesus came into the world.

However, Jesus did speak of heaven and earth passing away and his words never passing away (Matt 24:34–35). So, he seems to envisage a time when as heaven and earth pass away, parts of the law may be loosened and his followers no longer required to obey them. Jesus talks of heaven and earth passing away in the same discourse as he speaks of the coming of the Son of Man, when "the sun will be darkened, and the moon will not give her light, and the stars will fall from heaven, and the powers of the heavens will be shaken" (Matt 24:29). Here we have heaven and earth passing away. At this time, as heaven and earth pass away, various commands of the law may be loosened, but as Jesus affirms "my words will never pass away" (Matt 24:35). Although this is contentious, I believe that this prophecy of the coming of the Son of Man refers to the judgment of God in the destruction of the Jerusalem temple, which took place in AD 70.[37] (I believe that other

---

33. Davies and Allison, *Matthew*, 2:289.

34. France, *Matthew*, 181–91.

35. France (*Matthew*, 186–8) suggests that the real issue is whether Scripture can be invalidated, which it cannot, and that the exact way in which the commandments are interpreted (or laid aside in practice) is subordinate to the question of the authority of Scripture and the authority of Jesus. The problem with this is that it is not what the text says. It clearly states that commandments are not to be laid aside. France himself admits "Behavior is not excluded, of course . . ." (*Matthew*, 187).

36. As France acknowledges (*Matthew*, 185).

37. For a study of this kind of apocalyptic language and what it means, see Angel, *Chaos*. For scholars who argue for this understanding of the coming of the Son of Man

prophecies of the Son of Man, e.g., when he takes his throne before the nations [Matt 25:31–46] refer to the second coming). So, Jesus envisaged the loosening of commands of the law when the temple was destroyed.

This would make perfect sense at one level for many of the commands in the law concern the sacrificial system. Once there was no temple, there was no way in which these laws could obviously or literally be obeyed. The occasion of the destruction of the temple then makes sense as the occasion on which these laws are loosened. So, as John Calvin suggests, the literal meaning of the laws concerning "ceremonies" appears to pass away. He argues that their deeper significance finds its fulfillment in Christ.[38] Where Jesus speaks of the wine as his blood poured out for many, he uses sacrificial language and imbues his death with the significance of a sacrifice for the forgiveness of sins (Matt 26:28) in which he gives his life as a ransom instead of many (Matt 20:28).[39] So, in Matthew, Jesus envisages his death as a sacrifice in which he dies instead of others so that they may be forgiven. There would therefore be no need for the sacrificial regulations to be carried out after the temple had been destroyed as Christ had already died as a sacrifice for humanity.

Much as this might make some sense, there is no indication in Jesus' words that he limits the loosening of laws only to the sacrificial regulations. His words could easily suggest that he envisaged other laws also being loosened. Limits are certainly set on how far one can press the loosening of the commandments of the law by the teaching of Jesus as it will never pass away. For example, Jesus could not permit worshipping another God or making an idol (Exod 20:3–6; Matt 4:10). He would not permit making wrongful use of the name of the Lord by breaking oaths (Exod 20:7; Matt 5:33–37). He upheld honoring father and mother (Exod 20:12; Matt 15:4–9; 19:19). He prohibited murder (Exod 20:13; Matt 5:21–22; 19:18). He also prohibited adultery (Exod 20:14; Matt 5:27–30; 19:18). He would not permit stealing (Exod 20:15; Matt 19:18) or the bearing of false witness (Exod 20:16; Matt 19:18).[40] Given these facts, there is no way that anyone

---

in Matt 24:29–35, see Wright (*Victory of God*, 339–68) and France (*Matthew*, 896–931). For the opposing view, see Adams, *Stars Will Fall*.

38. Calvin, *Harmony*, 277–80.

39. Note in Matt 20:28, Jesus uses the word *anti* ("instead of") and not *hyper* ("on behalf of"). Jesus envisages his death as being instead of the death of the many. His death is substitutionary and sacrificial.

40. The list here is indicative and not exhaustive. It provides no evidence that Jesus permitted either coveting or Sabbath breaking!

can read the text with any honesty and say that Jesus only expected people to obey the commands to love God and their neighbor. When, for example, Calvin suggests that Jesus wants his disciples to keep the ten commandments, he seems to reflect what Matthew says about Jesus' teaching.[41] However, the question of how far Jesus expects commands on which he does not comment to be obeyed is more complex.

(Another complexity is this: if Jesus' death was a sacrifice for the forgiveness of sins and his body was the new temple (Matt 26:61, cf. John 2:19–21), then why did early Christians worship in the temple (e.g., Luke 24:53; Acts 3:1)? This is not the only oddity in the New Testament around observance of the commandments of the law and temple worship after the death and resurrection of Jesus. I sketch out an answer to the questions raised by these oddities in the appendix "Thoughts on Jesus, Paul, and the Law." I suspect that following through the argument I put out there may help find a way forward, not only on ethical issues on which Jesus did comment but also on the thorny issue of handling ethical issues on which Jesus did not comment directly.)

Matthew 5:17–20 suggest that Jesus required his followers to obey the law, or at least the parts of the law that he affirms in his teaching—his final interpretation of the law. This final interpretation of the law contains a number of the commandments of the Torah. So, Jesus' understanding of the law cannot be reduced to "love God, love your neighbor, and work out in your own experience what this means in practice." But this raises another problem: if Jesus teaches obedience to the commands of his law, how do we reconcile this teaching with the words and actions of Jesus in the Gospels where he seems to break the law? The Gospels present Jesus in conflict with his contemporaries over the law. They want to check out his faithfulness to the commandments (e.g., Matt 12:9, where some in the synagogue ask Jesus if it is lawful to heal on the Sabbath, assuming it is not). If Jesus acts in ways that break the law as some of his contemporaries understand it, does this mean that Jesus contradicts his words in Matt 5:17–20 by his words and actions elsewhere in the Gospels?

Did Jesus break the law?

Did Jesus break the law or teach breaking the law? Not really. The Gospels record debates with his Jewish contemporaries about his or his disciples'

---

41. Calvin, *Harmony*, 279.

actions and whether they are keeping the law or not. However, as we shall see below, in these debates neither Jesus nor the disciples actually break any of the commandments in the Torah. Where they break any law code, it seems more likely to have been the traditions of the Pharisees, which they created as a hedge around the law to prevent people getting anywhere near to breaking the law.[42]

The Mishnah (the collection of the teachings of the rabbis made around AD 200) talks of the prophets of Israel telling the men of the great assembly to make a fence, or hedge, around the Torah (m. 'Abot 1:1). Rabbi Akiba (c. AD 50–135) described *tradition* as a fence around the Torah (m. 'Abot 3.13). Tradition was the commentary that the rabbis had made on the commands of the Torah, to explain how they thought those commands were best obeyed. One reason for the commentary was to build in safeguards against breaking the law. For example, later tradition suggested that Moses himself added a day to the two days over which God called the Israelites to purify themselves at Sinai (Exod 19:10–15). Moses' reasoning was that if he added a day, fewer Israelites were likely to slip up. If the Israelites were aiming for three days' purity in all, more of them would manage the two days that God actually required ('Abot R. Nat. 2). The purpose of the extra commands was to enable Israel to be obedient to the law and so find God's blessing ('Abot R. Nat. 2). Sometimes this commentary on the laws written in the Torah might be referred to as the oral Torah. Although not all seem to have accepted the validity of this oral law, tradition has it that the great rabbis Hillel and Shammai both accepted it and that it had a central place in the teaching of the Pharisees and their successors, the rabbis ('Abot R. Nat. 15).[43]

42. I shall limit my study of possible places where Jesus broke the commandments of the Torah to the Gospel of Matthew, as this book is fundamentally a study of the Matthean portrait of Jesus. I shall endeavor to keep comments on other gospels limited to the footnotes.

43. Another point worth making before we examine Jesus' discussions and debates with his Jewish contemporaries is that his disagreements were not all with the Pharisees. Some were with Pharisees and others were with the scribes or the Herodians. Even the disciples of John the Baptist took issue with Jesus over the way he and his disciples practiced their faith. There can be an unpleasant tendency in the "comforting myths" to victimize the Pharisees as if they were the only people that disagreed with Jesus and to assume that they always and invariably did so. But they were not the only ones to disagree with him, and on at least one occasion Jesus praised their interpretation of the law (Matt 23:2–3): "The scribes and the Pharisees sit on Moses' seat. So, do and keep all the things they tell you, but do not act the way they do. Because they speak and they do not act." These words indicate that Jesus had respect for the teaching of at least some Pharisees.

The Jesus We Don't Want to Know

The first place in the Gospel narrative where Jesus seems to break the law is the story of the healing of the paralytic (Matt 9:2–8). On seeing the faith of the paralytic and those who brought him to Jesus, Jesus tells the paralytic that his sins are forgiven. This draws the criticism from some of the scribes that Jesus was blaspheming (Matt 9:3). They assume that only God has the right to forgive sins and that Jesus has arrogated this right to himself.[44] Although the law requires punishment for anyone who "blasphemes" (Lev 24:10–23; Num 15:30–31), it does not specify what blasphemy actually is, beyond misuse of the name of the Lord God.[45] The scribes

---

Certainly, the fact that Jesus does criticize the teachings of the Pharisees and Sadducees (Matt 16:11–12) stands in tension with this affirmation of the Pharisees' teaching. However, there seems to be little reason to deny this positive assessment of the Pharisees any validity at all simply because elsewhere in the Gospel Jesus criticizes them. The Gospel presents Jesus as making *both* assessments of the Pharisees and so suggests Jesus' view of them was more nuanced that we sometimes allow. (The seeming contradiction between this saying and that in Matt 16:11–12 is admittedly difficult. I find Davies and Allison's [*Matthew*, 3:270] view that the "all" in "do and keep *all* they tell you" is not to be taken literally attractive, given that Matthew uses "all" in this way elsewhere [e.g., Matt 2:3; 3:5] and that Jesus clearly thinks that at least some of their teachings are wrong [Matt 16:11–12]. Reading the "all" this way makes it easier to read both Matt 16:11–12 and Matt 23:2–3 together, rather than assuming that Matthew is a weak redactor who cleverly structures a neat literary piece together but accidently builds glaring contractions into one of his key themes, namely Jesus as true teacher of the law [similarly, Gundry, *Matthew*, 454–55]. However, this does not clear up all the complexities of Matt 23:2–3. Some try to "rescue" Jesus from meaning these words by suggesting either that they are said sarcastically [Talbert, *Matthew*, 257] or that Jesus simply does not mean what he says [Filson, *Matthew*, 243]. However, Jesus' teaching on, for example, marriage seems very close to that of Shammai [m. Giṭ. 9:10]. This makes it much easier to see how Jesus might have affirmed some teachings of the Pharisees in particular, and less easy to see how Jesus could really have been entirely sarcastic about them or simply not meant that they were ever in the right.) Those of us who tend to view Jesus' debates with his contemporaries as a "western" in which Jesus and his disciples are the cowboys and the Pharisees are the Indians, need to recognize that the Gospels present a more nuanced picture than this.

44. So, both Mark and Luke, who state the reason for the charge of blasphemy: "who can forgive sins except God alone?" (Mark 2:7; Luke 5:21). For this reading, see Davies and Allison, *Matthew*, 2:91; France, *Matthew*, 346; and Harrington, *Matthew*, 121. Interestingly, Luke adds the Pharisees to the scribes here—an awkward detail for any who suggest that Matthew focuses on conflict with the Pharisees (post Jamnia) and so adds them in conflict narratives where the other Synoptic evangelists do not place them.

45. The Mishnah states that someone may only be held liable for blasphemy if they fully pronounce the divine name, YHWH (m. Sanh. 7:5). Jesus has not blasphemed in this sense, but the fact that the Mishnah defines blasphemy in this way around AD 200, does not preclude the possibility that some scribes around AD 40 held a wider definition of blasphemy. So, I can see no good reason to reject the picture offered in Matthew—and surely the scribes are right that only God can forgive sins!

in the narrative offer further definition of blasphemy which is not found in the Torah, suggesting that a man forgiving sins constitutes blasphemy. Technically, however, Jesus did not break any commandment when he did this because the law nowhere says that it is blasphemy for a human being to forgive sins. More importantly, Jesus has been portrayed as "God with us" since the opening of the Gospel (Matt 1:23).[46] Consequently, as God, he does have the right to forgive sins. This is what Jesus means when he says that the Son of Man has authority to forgive sins on earth (Matt 9:6). Jesus identifies himself as the "Son of Man," a figure who appears in divine glory in the throne room of God in heaven and who is enthroned alongside God the Father (Dan 7:9–14).[47] So, not only has Jesus not broken any commandments but he has not arrogated any divine prerogatives to himself precisely because he is divine and they belong to him anyway. Moreover, the phrase Jesus uses to tell the man that he has been forgiven could very easily be read as suggesting that it is God who has forgiven this man his sins. Jesus says, "your sins are forgiven" (i.e., by God [Matt 9:2]), not "I forgive you your sins." So, any charge that Jesus has broken any commandment about blasphemy here simply will not stick.

---

46. Gundry, *Matthew*, 163.

47. I am more than aware of just how controversial this statement will be in some quarters, as the debates over the interpretation of the "Son of Man" sayings in the Gospels are far from solved to everybody's satisfaction. However, it remains a fact that the only person to use this title of Jesus in the Synoptic Gospels is Jesus himself, and that on a number of occasions he identifies himself with the "one like a son of man" of Dan 7:13–14 (e.g., Matt 24:30). The authors of the Synoptic Gospels use exactly the same Greek words (*ho huios tou anthrōpou*) in all the places where Jesus refers to himself as "the Son of Man," suggesting that they portray Jesus as referring to the same Son of Man every time he uses the phrase—and that this Son of Man is the one of Dan 7:13–14. In Daniel 7, this "one like a son of man" travels in clouds, which signify his divinity (see, Angel, *Chaos*, 99–110). The authors of the Synoptic Gospels develop the language of Daniel to further suggest that Jesus as Son of Man is divine (see, Angel, *Chaos*, 125–34). Therefore, I do not see the "Son of Man" indicating a semi-divine or a super-angelic being with whom Jesus identifies himself (so John and Adela Collins, *King and Messiah*) but as *actually* divine. I am aware that Jesus' Jewish contemporaries only believed in one God and so would have found both his suggestion that the Son of Man was a second divine figure in heaven and that he himself was this second divine figure difficult. This is precisely why, I believe, the high priest and Sanhedrin condemned him to death on a charge of blasphemy immediately after he identifies himself as the Son of Man sitting at the right hand of God and coming on the clouds of heaven (Matt 26:64–66). However, not even this can constitute breaking the law in Matthew as Jesus *rightly* identifies himself as the divine Son of Man. Far from constituting blasphemy, this is the self-revelation of God to his people.

The Pharisees approached Jesus' disciples and asked them why Jesus ate with tax collectors and sinners (Matt 9:11). Table fellowship was certainly an issue for the Pharisees. However, the Pharisees do not accuse Jesus of breaking the law here. Nor does he break any commandment found in the five books of the Torah. Jesus' response to the Pharisees' question is to point out that the sick need a doctor, not the fit. To justify his point, he quotes Hos 6:6: "I want mercy, not sacrifice" (Matt 9:13). Given that nobody in the conversation has mentioned anything to do with sacrifices, laws about sacrifice cannot be the point here. The point is mercy, specifically that God wants mercy shown to sinners—which is why Jesus eats with them, despite contemporary Pharisaic concerns about that. Neither Jesus nor the Pharisees suggest that anyone is breaking any commandment, nor that anyone should break any commandments. The Pharisees are concerned to honor God by being holy and Jesus wants to live out God's desire to show mercy. They disagree on how these things are worked out in practice, and nobody suggests breaking any laws.

The disciples of John the Baptist wonder why Jesus' disciples are not fasting when they and the Pharisees fast (Matt 9:14). The disciples of John probably followed the example of their master who was well known for his fasting (Matt 11:18; Luke 7:33). The Pharisees used to fast (see, for example, the Mishnaic tractate Ta'anit) and understood that the act of fasting had to be accompanied by true repentance (m. Ta'an. 2:1). There were regulations in the law about when all the people of Israel were obliged to fast, such as on the Day of Atonement (Lev 16:1–34). However, there is no suggestion in the text that either Jesus or his disciples are failing to observe one of these obligatory fasts.[48] So, Jesus' disciples are breaking no commandment. Nor is Jesus. In fact, Jesus is not accused of anything here—except possibly, by implication, of having spiritually wayward disciples. However, even that does not technically involve the breaking of any of the commandments in the law. Jesus has simply not required his disciples to follow the same spiritual disciplines as the disciples of John the Baptist and the Pharisees.

Jesus may have contracted ritual impurity when the woman with the hemorrhage touched him (Matt 9:20–22).[49] Although a plain reading of Lev 15:19 would certainly suggest that Jesus contracted impurity, he did not break the law. He did not touch her—she touched him. He would not have broken the law by contracting ritual impurity anyway. He would simply

---

48. Similarly, Davies and Allison, *Matthew*, 2:108–9.
49. Turner, *Matthew*, 259.

be ritually impure until the evening. Nothing in the text in Matthew suggests that Jesus did anything the law prohibited him from doing in a state of impurity. Something similar must be said of his touching the corpse of Jairus' daughter when he raised her from the dead (Matt 9:25). Touching a corpse made a person ritually impure (Lev 22:4; Num 5:2).[50] However, the Torah does not command that one shall not do this. It simply regulates what someone may and may not do in this state of ritual impurity and how long the impurity lasts. Jesus did not break the law by touching the corpse of Jairus' daughter or by the woman with the discharge touching him.[51]

There are two episodes in which some of Jesus' contemporaries suggested that he or his disciples broke Sabbath laws. One day walking through the cornfields, his disciples began to pluck ears of corn and eat them because they were hungry, and the Pharisees accused them of doing what was not lawful on the Sabbath (Matt 12:1–2). The law states that no harvesting should take place on the Sabbath (Exod 34:21). However, there is no command against plucking a few ears of corn.[52] The question of what constituted harvesting did come up and was discussed by Jews around the time of Jesus. Philo clearly thought that plucking of any kind of food was prohibited on the Sabbath (Moses 2:22). Later rabbis prohibited plucking on the Sabbath (y. Šabb. 7:2). So, the Pharisees do not question Jesus' disciples over any command in the law, as there was no command prohibiting plucking corn. They question his disciples over their *interpretation* of the command prohibiting harvesting on the Sabbath.[53] Jesus tackles their interpretation by building up an argument about what can be done on the Sabbath. First, he notes that David and his men were hungry and so ate the

---

50. Morris, *Matthew*, 232.

51. Sometimes people express the view that Jesus made the unholy holy by touching them in these stories. In the law, the sons of Aaron are made holy through being sprinkled with the blood of a sacrificed ram (Exod 29:19–21; similarly, Lev 6:24–30). Given that these laws relate specifically to the consecration of priests, I remain to be convinced by this idea, not least as I cannot see the evangelist making this point in his telling of these stories.

52. The term Jesus uses for plucking (Greek *tillō*) is never used of harvesting in the LXX (the Greek translation of the Old Testament). The term used in Exod 34:21 is *amētos*, a term unrelated to *tillō*. So, Matthew does not suggest that the disciples are harvesting or breaking the law. For a more detailed discussion of this issue, see Crossley, *Date*, 160–72.

53. Although there is no command in the Mishnah that specifically prohibits plucking food on the Sabbath, the fact that Philo discusses it and later rabbis do prohibit it makes it entirely plausible that at least some Pharisees at the time of Jesus thought that plucking contravened the law. For detailed discussion, see Crossley, *Date*, 160–62.

bread of the presence, which only priests were allowed to eat (Lev 24:5–9), implying they broke the law (Matt 12:4). (As the bread is changed and the old bread is eaten on the Sabbath [Lev 24:8–9], this must have happened on the Sabbath.) So, a great hero of the faith broke the Sabbath law for hunger. Second, Jesus points out that the law requires priests to sacrifice on the Sabbath (Num 28:9–10), which means that they are working and so violating the Sabbath commandment, but Jesus states that they are guiltless in this. The Mishnah regulates which parts of the Passover sacrifices can override Sabbath law (m. Pesaḥ 6:1–6), so the Pharisees clearly saw the problem facing priests being commanded to sacrifice on the Sabbath and they also worked out ways in which those sacrificing on the Sabbath might be held guiltless—so, the Pharisees could hardly disagree with Jesus here. Finally, Jesus asks, if Sabbath sacrifices were permitted for the sake of the temple cult, why would the Pharisees condemn the disciples for doing something that is not even against the law when something even more important than the temple was there (Matt 12:6–7)?[54] Jesus' argument does involve noting that David broke the Sabbath laws and arguing with the Pharisees on their own ground about which laws supersede which others when they clash or contradict each other. However, it does not involve either him or his disciples in breaking or recommending breaking the law. Rather, Jesus defends his disciples who have done something that violates the Pharisees' interpretation of the law *but not the law itself.*

The second Sabbath incident involves healing (Matt 12:9–14). Jesus enters the synagogue where there is a man with a withered hand and Jesus is asked whether it is lawful to heal on the Sabbath. He states that any of those gathered would rescue their sheep on the Sabbath if it fell into a ditch and argues that human beings are more important than sheep—concluding that it is lawful to do good on the Sabbath. The Essenes did not allow the rescuing of animals on the Sabbath (CD 11:13–14). This ruling, taken together with the Gospel text, suggests that there was a debate about whether animals might be rescued if they fell into a pit on the Sabbath. We can only assume that those in the congregation with Jesus that day loved their sheep, or the argument would not have worked. The Mishnah permits medicine on the Sabbath in the case of immediate danger to life, suggesting that otherwise treatment can wait until the Sabbath is over (m. Yoma 8:6),

---

54. Clearly, the something greater than the temple is Jesus (Davies and Allison, *Matthew*, 2:314), who is the "Son of Man" (i.e., a second divine person alongside the Ancient of Days in the throne room of heaven [Matt 12:8]).

which in turn suggests that within rabbinic and Pharisaic circles healing was not generally permitted on the Sabbath.[55] However, there is no commandment in the Torah that prohibits healing on the Sabbath. Therefore, when Jesus then healed the man with the withered hand he did not break any command in the law, although he did violate the fence that at least some Pharisees were building around the Torah.

It might be suggested that Jesus' sayings about his family contradict the commandment to honor one's father and mother (Exod 20:12; Deut 5:16).[56] On one occasion, Jesus was told his mother and brothers were waiting outside to speak to him and he responded "who are my mother and brothers?" answering his own question with the comment "whoever does my heavenly Father's will, *this person* is my brother or sister or mother" (Matt 12:46–50). The point Jesus makes was not new amongst Jews of his day. The law itself commanded that people should punish with death anyone who suggested they follow idols—even if they were their closest friends or relatives (Deut 13:1–11). The law also commends Levi for ignoring his father and his mother in order to follow God's commands (Deut 33:9).[57] Philo makes the same point when he discusses Deut 13:1–11 (*Spec. Laws* 1:58). Josephus has Moses say that the people of God should battle more jealously for God's commandments than for their own wives and children (*Ant.* 3:87). Jesus' point is that his true family are those who do his heavenly Father's will, and this makes him similar in this respect to the Torah, Philo, and Josephus. None of the Gospels have the scribes or Pharisees attack him

---

55. The Marcan and Lucan versions of the story have Jesus ask the question whether it is lawful to save life or kill on the Sabbath (Mark 3:4; Luke 6:9), which seem to reflect and extend the kind of ruling made in m. Yoma 8:6, which permits life-saving medicine on the Sabbath (Crossley, *Date*, 85). Mark and Luke also have Jesus heal Peter's mother-in-law on the Sabbath (Mark 1:29–31; Luke 4:38–39) and the same argument as given above applies—Jesus broke no commandment of the Torah by healing on the Sabbath.

56. Crossley (*Date*, 86) attributes this view to S. G. F. Brandon ("Date of Mark's Gospel," 138–9). In point of fact, Brandon says no such thing in this article. Wright (*Victory of God*, 278, 400–401) claims that the kind of statements Jesus made about his family were shockingly counter-cultural, although he does not claim that Jesus broke any of the commandments here. To be honest, however, the English-language/translation commentaries I have consulted (i.e., Albright and Mann, Davies and Allison, France, Green, Hagner, Hare, Harrington, Luz, Morris, Nolland, Talbert, and Turner) do not draw the conclusion that Jesus' words here contradict or break any commandment of the Torah. Nonetheless, for the sake of completeness, I include this in the discussion as a possible example of Jesus contradicting the law as clearly some people think some other people think this.

57. Davies and Allison, *Matthew*, 2:364.

for saying this, and why would they have done? Jesus has simply taught obedience to God. Given that we do not know what happened after Jesus had made his point either, it is difficult to argue that Jesus even disrespected his family here.[58] This saying is not evidence that Jesus broke with the Torah but that he was in line with both the law and some contemporary Jewish interpretation of it. The point he makes about obedience to the will of God would hardly have upset the Pharisees, and there is no evidence that it did.

Something similar may be said for two other sayings of Jesus. When preparing his disciples for mission in Israel, he made the following remarkable statement (Matt 10:34–39):

> Do not think that I have come to bring peace on the earth—I have not come to bring peace but a sword. For I have come to turn "a man against his father" and "a daughter against her mother" and "a bride against her mother-in-law" and "a man's enemies will be his household."[59] The person who loves father or mother more than me is not worthy of me, and the one who loves son or daughter more than me is not worthy of me. Whoever does not take up their cross and follow me is not worthy of me. Those finding their life will lose it, and those who lose their life for my sake will find it.

On another occasion, he tells his disciples that anyone who has left "brothers, or sisters, father or mother, or children" for his name's sake will receive one hundredfold and inherit eternal life (Matt 19:29). In both these sayings, Jesus teaches that those who place him above family ties will receive their reward from God—not least in the kingdom of heaven after the final judgment. However, Jesus does not talk of people doing the Father's will in these sayings but of their commitment to him. This could seem to be breaking the commandment to honor father and mother. However, again, the reason Jesus does not break the law in making these statements is because he *is* "God with us" (Matt 1:23), so commitment to him *is* commitment to God above family. Therefore, this teaching simply echoes the law and fulfills its demands.

Later in the Gospel narrative, the scribes and the Pharisees challenge Jesus because his disciples did not wash their hands before they ate (Matt 15:2). Note that they do not accuse Jesus, but his *disciples*. Jesus responds

---

58. Hare, *Matthew*, 145–46. For all we know, they are together. None of Matthew, Mark, or Luke use any verbal marker to suggest that what followed on happened immediately afterwards.

59. Jesus quotes Mic 7:6 here.

with the question: "Why do you transgress the commandment of God for the sake of your tradition?" (Matt 15:3). He identifies handwashing before eating as a Pharisaic tradition rather than a commandment. The rabbis did discuss ritual handwashing and what necessitated such handwashing (e.g., m. Ḥag. 2:2; m. Ḥul. 2:5; m. Yad. 3:2).[60] There are no commands in the law specifying that ordinary people should wash their hands before eating. Exodus 30:17–21 does require the priests to wash before entering the tabernacle or coming near the altar. However, this is far removed from ordinary people eating food at home. The Pharisees seem to have sought to bring the holiness of priests ministering before God in the temple into the way they ate at home.[61] So although they transgressed the fence or hedge the Pharisees were building around the law, neither the disciples nor Jesus broke *the law itself* by eating with unwashed hands.

Nor did Jesus speak against the law in his words: "nothing going into a person from the outside defiles them, but what comes out of the mouth—this defiles a person" (Matt 15:11). This could easily be read as Jesus annulling the commandments about not eating unclean food (Leviticus 11).[62] However, reading the text like this makes nonsense of the story. Before Jesus makes this comment, he criticizes the Pharisees for ignoring the commandment of God for the sake of their tradition (Matt 15:3). He shows how their teaching about dedicating gifts to God (which is not in the law) prevents them from obeying God's command to honor their parents (Exod 20:12; Deut 5:16), meaning they commit a sin for which God prescribes death as punishment (Exod 21:17).[63] He quotes Isa 29:13 to back up his point that the Pharisees are teaching their teachings as God's commands and so fail to honor God with their hearts and minds. To then state that

---

60. For a detailed discussion, see Crossley, *Date*, 183–85. Crossley discusses the Marcan parallel (Mark 7:1–23) and makes the important point that Mark ought to be taken alongside the later rabbinic material as evidence of the existence of a debate about handwashing before meals in the first century AD (given that some exclude the testimony of Mark and other evangelists as genuine historical evidence of the debate). I would add that, as another first-century AD document, Matthew also acts as a witness to such a discussion.

61. Neusner, *Politics to Piety*, 83.

62. So, e.g., Filson, *Matthew*, 178. Similarly, Hagner (*Matthew 14–28*, 432), although he notes that it is "far from Matthew's purpose" to undermine the Levitical food laws.

63. Technically, Exod 21:17 prescribes death for cursing father or mother and not specifically for failing to give them money they might need. However, unless Jesus understands this commandment to refer to people failing to support their parents, its presence in this text is superfluous. In interpreting texts, I prefer to assume that authors write coherently and so seek to interpret their texts accordingly.

none of the food laws in Leviticus 11 are valid would make Jesus as bad as the Pharisees, as he himself would be ignoring the commandments about unclean foods in the law to set up his own teaching. Possibly Jesus is speaking self-contradictory nonsense, but I prefer to give him the benefit of the doubt, assuming that there is a better understanding of the text. Two clues suggest there is. First, Peter reports that the Pharisees are scandalized by Jesus' comment (Matt 15:12). If Jesus had contradicted the law, we would expect everybody in the crowds Jesus addressed to be scandalized. If only the Pharisees were, then Jesus seems only to have offended them. Secondly, when Peter asks Jesus to explain the comment (or "parable") Jesus contrasts all the evil that comes out of the heart and mind with "eating with unwashed hands" (Matt 15:20). Jesus does *not* think he is talking about the food laws, but about whether people sin if they eat with unwashed hands. Therefore, his comment in v. 11 must be read in this context. He is saying that food eaten with unwashed hands does not defile, but all the evil that comes from the heart and mind defiles. Reading the text this way means that it makes perfect sense without any self-contradiction—which is important, as it is difficult to explain why Matthew would want to present the man he called Messiah, Son of God, and final interpreter of the law as a muddled and self-contradictory hypocrite. So again, Jesus does not criticize the law itself but only the fence that the Pharisees are building around the law.[64]

So, Jesus did not break the law. He and his disciples did break the extra instructions that some Pharisees were building as a hedge around the law, but Jesus did not break any of the commandments of the Torah. However, the dispute with the Pharisees over eating with unwashed hands raises another question: did Jesus teach breaking the law? He may not have broken the law himself and he may have defended his disciples from the charge

---

64. The parallel in Mark 7:1–23 contains the famous Marcan comment: "cleansing all foods" (Mark 7:19b). Whilst many have taken this to mean that Mark understood that Jesus broke with the food laws of Leviticus 11, such a reading is not necessary and makes nonsense of the text because of the self-contradiction in which it involves the Jesus of the Marcan narrative. Elaborate schemes of the history of the individual sections of Mark 7:1–23 are proposed (e.g., Bultmann, *History*, 17–18), which have been followed by commentators (e.g., Hooker, *Mark*, 173–74; Marcus, *Mark 1–8*, 447–48). However, none of these can explain adequately how the redactor of these text units could have been sufficiently stupid to tie them all together into the currently self-contradictory bundle in which we find them. There is no need for these schemes, which all fall foul of the mad redactor. If we simply acknowledge that "all" means different things in different situations (and very rarely means absolutely everything), then the "all foods" Mark refers to can simply be "all foods, whether eaten with washed or unwashed hands." Read this way, Mark 7:1–23 reads seamlessly. For a detailed argument, see Crossley, *Date*, 181–205.

that they broke the law, but this does not mean that he necessarily always taught that the law should be kept. Given that the comforting myths often suggest that Jesus taught people to break the law and do the loving thing instead, it is important that we ask the question and review the evidence.

Did Jesus teach others to break the law?

Some suspect that Jesus taught breaking the law in a series of six statements in the Sermon on the Mount, often referred to as "the antitheses" (Matt 5:21–48). They compare something that had been taught before (drawn from or related to the Torah) and an aspect of Jesus' teaching on the same subject. Each of the statements follows a similar formula, which is often translated "you have heard that it was said . . . but I say to you" (Matt 5:21–22, 27–28, 33–34, 38–39, 43–44), with a minor variation on the formula in Matt 5:31–32 ("it was also said . . . but I say to you").[65] Such English translations can make it sound as if Jesus disagreed with what had been said before and proposed something radically new instead. This impression would be mistaken. These translations can further this mistaken impression because of the way they translate the Greek word *de* (translated "but" in all these sayings but also translated "also" in Matt 5:31). The word *de* can mean "but," "and," or "also," and when it means "but" it does not necessarily imply a sharp contrast between two completely different things. So, we ought not to read these sayings as necessarily contrasting Jesus' teaching against the law. They follow Jesus' words: "Honestly, I tell you that unless your righteousness more than exceeds that of the scribes and the Pharisees, you will not enter the kingdom of heaven" (Matt 5:20). So, the context of these sayings suggests that they do not contradict the law but show the kind of *greater righteousness* Jesus wants his disciples to live out in their lives.

The first concerns the commandment not to commit murder (Matt 5:21–26), one of the ten commandments (Exod 20:13; Deut 5:17). Jesus teaches his followers that everyone who is angry with another disciple will be liable to judgment (Matt 5:22).[66] Presumably this judgment concerns some kind of community discipline (such as that Matthew describes in

---

65. These translations are given in the NRSV.

66. That Matthew has fellow believers in view seems to be the case from his use of *adelphos* to refer to fellow disciples. For the evidence, see Davies and Allison (*Matthew*, 1:512–13) despite their own reluctance to draw the conclusion to which the evidence they amass points.

Matt 18:15–22) as the judgment in the previous verse (Matt 5:21) refers to a human court and Jesus speaks of being liable to the Sanhedrin in the same verse (Matt 5:22).[67] Even so, divine judgment at the end of time is also in view, as Jesus also refers to the "Gehenna of fire" when he warns his disciples away from calling others "fool" (Matt 5:22). None of this in any way contradicts the commandment "do not murder." Nor does Jesus' advice on how to make up with another disciple in the following verses (Matt 5:23–26). Jesus does not contradict the law in this saying.

The second saying concerns the command not to commit adultery (Matt 5:27–30), the seventh of the ten commandments (Exod 20:14; Deut 5:18). Jesus teaches that every man who looks at a woman in order to feed his lust for her has committed adultery in his mind and will. He prohibits feeding sexual attraction to people who are off-limits by virtue of either himself or the woman being married. The issue at stake is feeding the mind and heart with lust for someone who is off-limits.[68] Both the original commandment and Jesus' teaching prohibit adultery. Neither prohibits healthy sexual attraction or the excitement and joy that comes with that. Instead, Jesus' teaching prohibits the kind of behavior that fosters and feeds instances of sexual attraction that might endanger marriage commitments. (In case this needs stating, this commandment does not refer to the mutual sexual attraction of two unmarried people.) When Jesus goes on to talk about your right eye and right hand causing you to sin, he refers to behaviors a man might use to act out this unhealthy and off-limits attraction, e.g., visually and through masturbation—why else refer to the right hand? (Again, in case this needs stating, Jesus does not condemn masturbation itself here, simply acting out off-limits sexual attractions through masturbation.)[69]

---

67. Davies and Allison (*Matthew*, 1:512) pose the difficulty: "one wonders how anger can be judged by a human court." This should not really cause difficulty as community leaders deal frequently (sometimes daily!) with issues arising from anger, seeking resolution to the anger, the problems it causes, and the issues giving rise to it. In the light of this, Jesus' instruction on community discipline in Matthew 18 seems ample answer to the problem they pose.

68. This is clear from the Greek, which uses a *pros to* construction, which denotes purpose and the idea of committing adultery in the heart, as the heart is the seat of the will in Hebrew thinking, the place where we make our decisions. Jesus refers to intentional following up of desires for someone, which involves thinking it through and doing it deliberately. Similarly, Nolland, *Matthew*, 236.

69. See Davies and Allison, *Matthew*, 1:525–26 (against, e.g., Nolland, *Matthew*, 238 n.166). For a detailed discussion of the text, see Angel, "God Talk."

The Jesus You *Really* Didn't Know

Nothing Jesus says here contradicts the commandment not to commit adultery.

Jesus comes closer to contradicting the law when he speaks of divorce (Matt 5:31–32). The Torah makes provision for a man to divorce his wife (Deut 24:1–4) and on first sight, Jesus' saying that any man who divorces his wife makes her commit adultery and whoever marries a divorced woman commits adultery seems to contradict this provision. The law required that a man give his former wife a certificate of divorce to protect her from the charge of adultery if she married another man (which would be an economic necessity for most women). Jesus does not seem to recognize the validity of such a certificate as he states that she commits adultery (i.e., against her original husband) if she married another man, and that any man who marries such a divorced woman also commits adultery (against her original husband).[70]

Jesus gives his reasoning for his view later in the Gospel (Matt 19:3–9). The Pharisees come to check him out on his interpretation of the law. They ask him whether it is lawful for a man to divorce his wife for any cause (Matt 19:3). There was discussion amongst the rabbis as to what constituted sufficient reason for divorce. Shammai said only for adultery where Hillel permitted divorce even for cooking him a bad meal (m. Giṭ. 9:10). They were interpreting the law about divorce in Deut 24:1, which permitted a man to divorce his wife if he found "something indecent" about her. The Pharisees in the Gospel story wanted to know Jesus' understanding of the words "something indecent" and so what he thought would constitute proper grounds for divorce. Given that marriages in the ancient world broke down, as they do today, and that the law permitted divorce (Deut 24:1–4), Jesus' response is surprising. He goes to the law to undercut the law. Rather than giving a straight answer to the question of whether the "something indecent" might refer to anything or adultery, he asks the Pharisees whether they have read the texts about the divine institution of marriage in the Torah. He quotes Gen 1:27 ("the Creator from the beginning made them male and female") and Gen 2:24 ("on account of this a man shall leave father and mother and be joined to his wife, and the two shall become one flesh"). On the basis of this story about how the Creator instituted marriage from the beginning, he asserts that no one should split apart what God has joined together (Matt 19:6). In response to their understandable question as to why Moses then permitted divorce, Jesus states

---

70. Talbert, *Matthew*, 84

that Moses permitted divorce on account of people's hard-heartedness (Matt 19:8). He does not deny the validity of the commands of Deut 24:1–4 but teaches another way, that of lasting marriage, which he justifies by arguing this was how God made marriage in the first place—as stated in the law. So, Jesus offers an explanation from the law as to why he will not engage in the Pharisaic debates about Deut 24:1–4 as well as offering a justification for the permission the law gives to divorce. After all this, he gives what sounds remarkably like an answer to the original question.[71] He claims that whoever divorces his wife *except for sexual immorality* and marries another, commits adultery (Matt 19:9; cf. 5:32).[72] Thus, he permits divorce in cases of sexual immorality. The debates around the interpretation of this verse are extensive.[73] Whatever one makes of the various disputed points, it may be safely said that Jesus here is nowhere near as lenient as Hillel and is at least as strict as Shammai.[74] So, Jesus is stricter than the Pharisees (or at least as strict as the stricter Pharisees) in his interpretation of the law. Given that he argues from the law in Genesis to justify his interpretation of the law

---

71. Similarly, Nolland, *Matthew*, 775.

72. The Greek word *porneia* means sexual immorality but is often translated adultery here. For a defense of this translation and interpretation, see Davies and Allison, *Matthew*, 1:529–31. For a defense of the view that Jesus here refers to proscribed marriages, see Fitzmyer, *Advance the Gospel*, 86–97 (whose arguments are noted by, e.g., Harrington [*Matthew*, 87–88, 273–74]). This view suggests that "except for sexuality immorality" refers to cases of marriage where the law prohibits persons in that kind of relationship from marrying each other. The force of Jesus' exception is then "those who are prohibited by God's law from marrying may divorce as their marriages were never proper marriages in the eyes of God."

73. There are various points of contention here, including: (i) the meaning of *porneia* (sexual immorality), on which see the previous footnote; (ii) whether Jesus does actually permit divorce of valid marriages; (iii) whether Jesus permits remarriage after legitimate divorce. On (ii), the argument that the exception clause refers only to marriages that are not permitted (see Lev 18:6–18 and the note above) suggests that Jesus does not permit divorce in the case of marriages between people who are permitted to marry. On (iii), some argue that the word order suggests that Jesus only permits divorce and not remarriage because the exception clause "except for sexual immorality" occurs after the words "divorces his wife" but before "and marries another," suggesting the words about remarriage are not covered by the exception (e.g., Wenham, "Matthew and Divorce"). Others argue that the issue cannot be decided on considerations of word order alone and take the exception clause to refer to divorce and remarriage, not least because rabbinic Judaism did not conceive of divorce without freedom to remarry, see m. Giṭ. 9:3 (e.g., Davies and Allison, *Matthew*, 3.17; Turner, *Matthew*, 462–63; France, *Matthew*, 211–13, 720; similarly, Nolland, *Matthew*, 243–47, 774).

74. So, e.g., Hagner, *Matthew 14–18*, 549. See also comments by France, *Matthew*, 208–11.

The Jesus You *Really* Didn't Know

in Deuteronomy 24, he does not want to break the law. Nor does he think he does so.

The fourth of the so-called antitheses concerns swearing oaths (Matt 5:33–37). Jesus states that his hearers have heard it said: "do not swear falsely but fulfill your oaths for the Lord's sake" (Matt 5:33) before he goes on to teach his disciples not to make oaths.[75] Unlike his teaching on murder and adultery (Matt 5:21–30), Jesus does not cite any particular commandment here.[76] So technically, he cannot be accused of teaching against a command he has not cited. Nevertheless, there are commandments in the law about making sure you fulfill any vows you make in the name of the Lord (e.g., Lev 19:12; Num 30:3–15; Deut 23:21–23).[77] However, none of these commandments require people to make oaths.[78] The commandments in Numbers and Deuteronomy simply outline the responsibilities of people

---

75. I translate *tō kyriō* as a dative of interest—unlike most commentators I have consulted (e.g., Davies and Allison, *Matthew*, 1:534; Luz, *Matthew 1–7*, 260; Nolland, *Matthew*, 249). Hence the translation "for the Lord's sake" rather than "to the Lord." This means that both halves of Matt 5:33b concern the same issue. By translating the "to the Lord," Jesus' words seem to move from oaths in the name of the Lord to oaths promising something to the Lord (e.g., Nolland, *Matthew*, 249), and they disagree on whether "you shall fulfill your vows to the Lord" restricts the sense of "you shall not swear falsely" only to vows to God (so, e.g., Hagner, *Matthew 1–13*, 127) or not (so, e.g., Nolland, *Matthew*, 249). There is good reason for believing that the whole of Matt 5:33–37 refers to oaths made in the name of the Lord in which something is promised to another, regardless of whether it is promised to another human person or to God. Matthew 5:33b talks of making good on ones oaths, so they cannot refer to oaths to prove innocence. These are promisory oaths. Nor can they be to God alone as "let your word be 'yes, yes' or 'no, no'" (Matt 5:37a) reads much more easily as referring to an oath made to another human person than to God. So, Jesus' words make perfect sense as they stand. Matthew 5:33b just needs reading as a dative of interest.

76. The verb Jesus uses, "break an oath" (Greek *epiorkidzō*) does not actually occur in the LXX, the Greek translation of the Old Testament.

77. For Lev 19:12 as referring specifically to taking oaths, see Milgrom, *Leviticus 17–22*, 1632–36. Other texts commentators list as Old Testament teaching on oaths, e.g., Ps 50:14; Zech 8:17 (see Davies and Allison, *Matthew*, 1:533–34; Harrington, *Matthew*, 88; Morris, *Matthew*, 123; Hagner, *Matthew 1–13*, 127; Gundry, *Matthew*, 91–92; France, *Matthew*, 214; Turner, *Matthew*, 172; Talbert, *Matthew*, 84) are not relevant here. Exodus 20:7 refers to taking the name of the Lord in vain, which is blasphemy rather than failing to fulfill vows. The other texts are not commandments in the law, i.e., the Torah.

78. The same must be said of the rash oath (Lev 5:4 [on which see Milgrom, *Leviticus 1–16*, 299–307]), the vow of Lev 27:2 (on which see Milgrom, *Leviticus 23–27*, 2367–80), and the vow of the Nazirite (Num 6:2 [on which see Levine, *Numbers 1–20*, 218]). In none of these cases does the law command the oath or vow to be made. It simply regulates what should happen once such an oath or vow has been made.

who make oaths. The commandment in Leviticus demands that nobody makes an oath in the name of the Lord which they then fail to keep because this would desecrate God's holy name. Jesus' teaching on oaths surely helps fulfill this commandment by preventing people from swearing oaths they will not keep.[79] The law itself taught that there was nothing wrong with refraining from making an oath (Deut 23:22). So, Jesus hardly contradicts the law here. He upholds it by teaching people not to make oaths and so end up in the situation which the law commands them not to end up in, i.e., breaking their oaths that they have made in the name of the Lord God Almighty.

Reading this teaching on oaths, some scholars suggest that Jesus comes close to breaking parts of the Torah, which commanded people to make oaths (e.g., Exod 22:10; Num 5:19–22).[80] However, Jesus does not seem to have these oaths in mind. There are two kinds of oaths: oaths made in the name of the Lord, which promise something to somebody ("swearing to give something"), and oaths made to prove innocence ("swearing you did not do it"). The laws in Exod 22:10 and Num 5:19–22 concern making oaths to prove innocence. Exodus 22:10 concerns two people arguing over who bears the responsibility for the loss of or damage to an animal which one of them left with the other for safekeeping. They both make an oath before the Lord to decide the case.[81] Numbers 5:19–22 concerns the oath a woman would take to clear herself of a charge of adultery brought against her by her husband.[82] Neither of these cases involves making an oath in which something is promised to anyone in the name of the Lord God. The oaths Jesus talks about in Matt 5:33–37 involve making some kind of promise in the name of the Lord, otherwise his comment "but fulfill your vows for the Lord's sake" makes no sense. So, the oaths Jesus talks about are ones where people are swearing to give something in the name of the Lord and do not concern any oath made to prove innocence.[83] Therefore, his teaching on oaths does not break any commandment of the Torah.

In the fifth "antithesis," Jesus says "you have heard it said 'an eye for an eye' and 'a tooth for a tooth'" before he goes on to teach turning the other cheek (Matt 5:38–42). The law does say "an eye for an eye, a tooth for a

---

79. Similarly, Harrington, *Matthew*, 88.
80. E.g., Nolland, *Matthew*, 252; France, *Matthew*, 215.
81. Propp, *Exodus 19–40*, 246–51.
82. Levine, *Numbers 1–20*, 196–97.
83. Betz, *Sermon*, 263–66.

tooth" (Exod 21:24; Lev 24:20; Deut 19:21), but what the law says may be more complex than it first appears.[84] Leviticus 24:20 forms part of a story in which the phrase is quoted as a principle of justice, not as a code of required punishments (Lev 24:10–23).[85] Deuteronomy 19:21 uses "eye for eye" as a principle to justify meting out the punishment on false witnesses that their lying in court would have had the accused suffer, and so also to act as a deterrent against perjury. In both instances, the words "an eye for an eye, a tooth for a tooth" are used as a principle to justify proportionate punishment. Exodus 21:22–25 specifies "life for life, eye for eye, tooth for tooth, hand for hand, foot for foot, burn for burn, wound for wound, stripe for stripe" as the punishments for any harm that might have been inflicted on a pregnant woman who was physically injured by people fighting.[86] However, immediately after this, the law commands that a slave-owner must release his slave by way of compensation if he blinds the eye or knocks out the tooth of one of his slaves (Exod 21:26–27), which demonstrates that the law did not require in all instances an actual eye for an eye.[87] So, the Torah

84. There are two ideas I do not address above as neither seems to me to hold water. First, some suggest that the *lex talionis* ("eye for eye") was given to limit the extent of retaliation and Jesus continues this limitation of violence in his teaching, so upholding the law (e.g., Davies and Allison, *Matthew*, 1:542). This view is untenable as the evidence does not support the idea that the *lex talionis* was used to limit violence but evolved as a replacement of monetary compensation as justice became the business of central authorities in society rather than the business of individuals agreeing privately recompense for grievances (see Propp, *Exodus 19–40*, 228). Second, others argue that Jesus is in line with the law as what he does with the *lex talionis* resembles the interpretation of some Jewish contemporaries (e.g., Crossley, *Date*, 102–3 [cf. Josephus, *Ant.* 4.280]). However, as Jesus himself distinguishes between the law and contemporary interpretation, clearly understanding the law to be God's will and sometimes setting this against contemporary interpretation, this is not a secure argument. It simply produces a mildly incoherent Jesus who speaks out against ignoring the law in favor of contemporary interpretation and then does precisely this himself.

85. The story concerns a man whose mother was an Israelite and whose father was Egyptian. Having had a fight with an Israelite, this man of mixed religious background blasphemed. Moses sought God, who revealed his judgment: that the man should be put to death; that all blasphemers should be put to death; that those who kill people should die; that those who kill animals should make restitution; and that those who maim others should receive the same injury—with the principle of an eye for and eye and so on being given as a justification for this.

86. Propp, *Exodus 19–40*, 231.

87. I cannot agree with Propp (*Exodus 19–40*, 232) that "to release a severely crippled slave would be no favor." Without diminishing the loss of an eye or a tooth, people with only one eye still have vision and the loss of one tooth does not do significant harm to the body. Therefore, the compensation this law ensures for the slave should not be lightly

uses "eye for eye, tooth for tooth" as a principle of justice, and as actual punishments, as well as commanding that in certain instances compensation must be made rather than meting out such a punishment. Therefore, any examination of whether Jesus teaches breaking the law here must involve some assessment of what Jesus understood by the words "eye for eye, tooth for tooth."

Given that Jesus does not elaborate on what he means by these words, we can only work out what he meant (if we can do so at all) from examining his reply: "but I tell you not to set yourselves up against an evil person" (Matt 5:39).[88] Jesus then outlines four or five cases of how to behave in response to evildoers: offer your left cheek to the person who slaps you on the right; leave your outer garment for the person who sues you for your inner garment; go two miles with the soldier who commandeers your services for one mile; give to those who ask, and do not turn away from those who want to borrow.[89] Only one of these examples concerns physical harm and thus possibly a "like for like" physical punishment as required by a literal understanding of "eye for eye, tooth for tooth."[90] The fact that the other four examples do not concern physical harm makes it extremely unlikely that Jesus cites "eye for eye, tooth for tooth" to comment on laws

---

dismissed. Even though there seems to be agreement amongst some commentators that this compensation is of a lesser form (so also Durham, *Exodus*, 324), I personally find it difficult to grasp how slaves in ancient Israel might prefer to see their owner lose one tooth than gain their freedom.

88. For the reading and translation "evil person," see Betz (*Sermon*, 281), who argues that the context (i.e., the following vv. 39–42) specifies how you act towards various categories of evildoer, which makes translating *tō ponerō* as the devil or an evil in general most unlikely. Davies and Allison (*Matthew*, 1:543) read the word "evildoer" and the following verses similarly. I have to demur from their interpretation at one point, however. I cannot understand why Jesus could have classed the poor and needy as evildoers because they asked for what they needed (presumably) when Jesus teaches caring for the poor. So, I am not convinced that either Jesus or Matthew had in mind a particular class of really evil beggars and borrowers here.

89. For further details on the nature of each of the four or five examples, see Betz, *Sermon*, 280–93; Davies and Allison, *Matthew*, 1:538–48. Some commentators see four examples, others see five. It all depends on whether you read v. 42 as one example in two parts ("give and do not refuse") or two examples.

90. Please note "possibly." The fact that the person is struck on the right cheek makes it most likely that this is a back-handed strike (Davies and Allison, *Matthew*, 1:543). The Mishnah rules exactly what monetary compensation should be given for such a strike (m. B. Qam. 8:6), four hundred *zuz*. Although the Mishnah was compiled later than Jesus, it is possible that at the time of Jesus such a strike received monetary compensation rather than "strike for strike."

about meting out physical punishments that reflect the original crime.[91] Another oddity concerns the second example, which does refer to seeking justice in court, but the person whom Jesus addresses appears to have done wrong because they are being sued: "if someone wants to sue you for your inner garment" (Matt 5:40). For Jesus' words to make any sense here, he must assume that these people are using the words "eye for eye, tooth for tooth" as an excuse for revenge on those who are bringing them to court.[92] The other three examples have nothing to do with violent crimes, seeking justice, or the courtroom. So, Jesus does not seem to be using "eye for eye" to introduce his teaching on appropriate punishments for violent crimes, or to discuss the principles of the legal system or issues of compensation for violent crimes.

The breadth of the issues covered suggests that Jesus cites "eye for eye, tooth for tooth" in order to establish a principle of generosity for living. It would be a mistake to assume that this has nothing at all to do with the legal system, as the first example does address someone who has suffered physical violence. However, the second addresses someone who is on the wrong side of the law and asks the same attitude from them. The third teaches generosity to someone who would very likely have had political objections to helping a soldier of an enemy occupying force but would have no recourse to take legal action against them.[93] It takes the issue beyond the law court and out into the politics of wider society. Jesus' teaching on giving and lending simply widens the whole issue out further, specifically to how we use our money in the face of those who are poor—and has nothing whatsoever to do with establishing justice in court.[94]

---

91. Nolland, *Matthew*, 257.

92. Similarly, Nolland, *Matthew*, 257.

93. I assume along with others that Matt 5:41 has Roman soldiers in mind (Harrington, *Matthew*, 89; Davies and Allison, *Matthew*, 1:546–47; Luz, *Matthew 1–7*, 273; France, *Matthew*, 221). I am not sure that the general thrust of Jesus' teaching here would change substantially if Jesus had been referring to the terrorist movements of his day.

94. The fact that Jesus widens the scope of his discussion beyond the courtroom in the third example encourages me to read the final examples as taking the whole issue wider still. The general thrust of Jesus argument seems to be: this does not simply refer to a wronged party in court, but the attitudes of the wrongdoer in court too, and how we act politically in wider society, and even in our interpersonal relationships beyond issues of legal process and politics. This is why I do not read those asking for something as evildoers, let alone some kind of evildoer whose crime has something specific to do with the operation of the *lex talionis* in the legal sphere. Jesus starts with court and evildoers but only to make his point about our attitude of generosity governing all we do in all

So, Jesus talks about "eye for eye" and "tooth for tooth" as if people were using these phrases as principles for living. In each example Jesus gives, he teaches outrageous generosity: if someone hits you, let them hit you again, even though you could sue them for a lot of money; if you are being sued, give them more than they are asking in court; if a hated enemy soldier requires some service of you, give them twice as much as they ask for; and if anyone at all asks for help, help them. At one level, Jesus does challenge the attitude people can bring to the justice system and for which the law made provision (punishments that fit the crime). However, as compensation (instead of literal "eye for eye") was built into the law, Jesus cannot be accused of breaking the law unless we are equally willing to accuse the law of breaking the law. In teaching outrageous generosity, again Jesus can hardly be accused of breaking the law. The law required people to leave part of the crop for poor people to come, take, and eat as they wanted (Lev 19:9–10; 23:22; Deut 24:19–22)—and this on top of the tithe from the field (Deut 14:22). Given that ancient Jews recognized that some poor were undeserving (e.g., Prov 6:10–11; 10:4; 14:23; 20:13; 23:20–21; 24:33–34; 28:19), this legal requirement is outrageously generous.[95] (The law does not limit the generosity to the widow, orphan, and deserving poor.) Nor does Jesus simply dispense with the idea of justice: his teaching on murder (Matt 5:21–26) assumes both the operation of law courts and the judgment of God at the end of time. So again, Jesus cannot really be accused of breaking the law in his teaching on "eye for eye, tooth for tooth."

In the sixth and final "antithesis," Jesus addresses the following saying people had heard: "'you will love your neighbor' and hate your enemy" (Matt 5:43–48). By way of contrast Jesus teaches that we should love our enemies and pray for those who persecute us. His reasoning is that if God can bless both those who follow and those who reject him, his people can bless both those who love them and those who mistreat them. Jesus does not teach anyone to break the law in doing this. The law clearly says "love

---

spheres of life.

95. The book of Proverbs was written well before the time of Jesus (Fox, *Proverbs 1–9*, 6) and was admittedly not canonical, although it was clearly used by Jews of the period (for use of Proverbs by, e.g., Sirach, see Fox, *Proverbs 1–9*, 6; Skehan and Di Lella, *Ben Sira*, 43–45). Just in case the reader doubts my point or evidence here, Judaism more contemporary to Jesus also recognized the idea that some poor were poor on account of their own irresponsibility (e.g., Tob 4:13) despite widespread teaching on helping the poor. For date of Tobit and its use by Jews contemporary to Jesus, see Fitzmyer, *Tobit*, 50–54.

your neighbor" (Lev 19:18). However, it nowhere says "hate your enemy."[96] Not even in instructions for warfare (e.g., Deut 20:10–18) does the law command that people should hate their enemies. Even if we were to construe from such instructions that the law required hatred of enemies, we would have to balance that against the foundational calling of Israel to be a blessing to the nations (Gen 12:1–3). Given that the call to Abraham and his descendants to bless all nations lies right at the heart of the identity of the people of God and their story in the Torah, it would be difficult to argue that Jesus breaks the law by commanding people to love their enemies.

In not one of these "antitheses" does Jesus teach breaking the law—or if he does in the case of divorce, he does so on the basis of upholding the law. In these discussions of the law and areas of life in which the law legislates, Jesus seems keen to establish the kind of righteousness to which he believes God really calls those who follow him. Immediately before the "antitheses," Jesus tells his followers they will not enter the kingdom of heaven unless their righteousness exceeds (Greek *perisseusē*) that of the scribes and Pharisees (Matt 5:20). In the final "antithesis," Jesus asks the question: "and if you only love your brothers, what extra (Greek *perisson*) are you doing?" (Matt 5:47). The idea of a better righteousness than the scribes and Pharisees brackets the whole section in which Jesus discusses the law and ideas within it.[97] Jesus' point is not that we should break the law but that we should live it out better than the scribes and Pharisees.

On one occasion, a disciple asked to delay following Jesus in order to bury his father. Jesus' response was "leave the dead to bury their dead" (Matt 8:22). Some see Jesus requiring this man to break the commandment to honor his father (Exod 20:12; Deut 5:16). Although the law did not specifically command that children must bury their fathers, the cultural expectation was that they would and that this was an important duty.[98] Very likely "the dead" who were to do the burying were the spiritually dead— that is, those who did not follow Jesus.[99] So Jesus tells the man to leave the burial of his father to those who will not follow him. Given that Jesus

---

96. Davies and Allison, *Matthew*, 1:549. Some think that this "antithesis" is aimed at the Essenes, who taught that true followers of God ought to hate all the sons of darkness (1QS 1:10–11)—e.g., Harrington, *Matthew*, 89.

97. Davies and Allison, *Matthew*, 1:559.

98. The Mishnah exempts a man from reciting the *Shema* if his dead need burying (m. Ber. 3:1).

99. Davies and Allison, *Matthew*, 2:56 (for the use of dead in this way in contemporary Jewish literature, see n.168).

tells him to leave the spiritually dead to bury "*their own*" dead, he must be referring to other members of this disciple's family burying this man's father—not suggesting that the father lies unburied.[100] Even so, this would still be shocking if the man's father had just died. However, this is unlikely to be the situation. If he had done so, and the man really had the desire to honor his father he appears to have, then this man would hardly be following Jesus around with the rest of the crowds. He would be keeping vigil over the body of his father and burying it.[101] In Middle Eastern idiom, the phrase "bury my father" means look after my father until the end of his life and then bury him. So, this disciple was asking Jesus to stay with his father for the remainder of his life and then come and follow him.[102] In this context, Jesus' reply may cut across cultural norms of remaining with the family but it does not require a disciple to break the fifth commandment or any family burial duties it might seem to entail. If this disciple did respond to Jesus' call to follow that day, he may have had the opportunity to return later in life and fulfill his filial duty to bury his father.

On another occasion, the Pharisees and the Herodians approached Jesus and asked him whether it was lawful to pay taxes to Caesar (Matt 22:15–22). The political cleft stick in which this left Jesus is well known. Answering that it was lawful would make him unpopular with the people, as they resented Roman rule and taxation.[103] Answering that it was not lawful might get him in trouble with Rome. In terms of our question, whether or not Jesus taught others to break the law, the issue is irrelevant. Much as many in Judaea at the time might have found it very difficult to believe that paying taxes to Rome could align with the will of God, the fact remains that it was not prohibited in the Torah. Jesus' response (however we read it) does not involve teaching anyone to break any commandment in the law.

The result of this survey has to be that Jesus did not really break the law.[104] Nor did he teach others to break the law. The closest he gets to this is his conversation about divorce law with the Pharisees, where Jesus justifies his position that no one should separate two people whom God has joined

---

100. Crossley, *Date*, 107.
101. Bailey, *Peasant Eyes*, 26.
102. Bailey, *Peasant Eyes*, 26–27; Dunn, *Jesus Remembered*, 504.
103. For further details, see Davies and Allison, *Matthew*, 3:215–16.

104. I have excluded from this review a discussion of Matt 11:13 "the law and the prophets prophesied until John" as I cannot see its relevance. Jesus here talks of a prophetic function of the law, not of its legal function in specifying how the people of God should behave. Therefore, it is irrelevant to this discussion.

together *from the Torah itself*. Jesus seeks to uphold the law. Although Jesus does not break or teach breaking the law, he does disagree with the Pharisees over the hedge they were building around the law. He makes strong criticisms of the traditions they added to the Torah. On the other hand, his own teaching of the Torah was not always so different from that of the Pharisees. On marriage, comparisons may be legitimately made between Jesus and Shammai who may not have been that far apart on the legitimacy of divorce. Interestingly, his strongest words are reserved for those who disobey the commandments of God in order to uphold the traditions they are building up around the Torah. In these criticisms, he makes it quite clear that he is radically committed to obedience to God's commandments. So, the picture of Jesus as the one who breaks the law in the name of love holds no water because Jesus did not break the law. Nor did he teach others to break the law, which puts paid to the idea that he taught others to do the loving thing instead of obeying the law. Instead, he was radically, if not fiercely, committed to obedience to the commandments of God.

Did Jesus keep the law?

When thinking about Jesus' attitude to and views of the law, there is another question which needs asking. To ask the question "did Jesus break the law?" is only to explore half of the issue. It points out where Jesus may have broken or been perceived by others to have broken the law. This only gives one side of the story on whether Jesus kept the law. It does not explore the places where Jesus tried to keep the law or where he encouraged others to do the same. So, the next question that needs asking is "did Jesus keep the law?" or, at the very least, "in what instances, if any, did Jesus keep the law or encourage others to keep the law?"

Following the Sermon on the Mount is a story of Jesus healing a leper (Matt 8:1–4). The leper asks to be cleansed and Jesus stretches out his hand to touch and cleanse him. Jesus then instructs the ex-leper to show himself to the priest and to make the offering commanded in the law of Moses (Lev 14:1–32). Jesus upholds the law here because he instructs the ex-leper to fulfill the requirements of the law. Incidentally, strictly speaking, Jesus' touching the leper does not involve him in infringing any commandment in the law.[105] Touching someone who has ritual uncleanness would make someone ritually unclean (Lev 5:3) but did not involve transgression of

---

105. Davies and Allison, *Matthew*, 2:13.

a commandment of the Lord.[106] This kind of ritual impurity did require cleansing to safeguard the temple from impurity but only incurred sin if the ritually impure person did not seek purification when they knew they should.[107] So Jesus might have contracted ritual impurity but would not have transgressed a commandment in the law. Given that he told the leper to obey the laws of ritual purification, there is no reason to suppose that he would have objected to undergoing ritual purification himself.[108] So in upholding the laws of ritual purification by instructing the leper to show himself to the priest, Jesus kept the law.

In one very basic way, Jesus appears to have kept the law daily in the way he dressed. The Gospel narrative notes that sick people begged him to touch even the fringe of his cloak and as many as did this were healed (Matt 14:35–36). His cloak or outer garment had a fringe or tassels. Jewish men were commanded in the Torah to wear a fringe or tassels on their garments to remind them of the commandments of God and not follow the evil desires of their own hearts (Num 15:38–39; Deut 22:12).[109] Jesus clearly obeyed this commandment as a reminder that he should follow the commands of God rather than any evil desires. Given his prayer in the garden of Gethsemane, "yet not what I want but what you want" (Matt 26:39), his following this commandment either reflected or contributed to his spirituality

---

106. Milgrom (*Leviticus*, 307–13) helpfully explains that the cases of impurity requiring purification in Lev 5:1–13 are to be distinguished from those requiring purification in Lev 4:1–35 precisely because these latter cases are incurred through transgression of a prohibitive commandment of the Lord (Lev 4:2), which is clearly not the case in Lev 5:1, as nothing there is said of transgressing such commands. Some commentators on the Gospel story (e.g., Harrington, *Matthew*, 113; Morris, *Matthew*, 189; France, *Matthew*, 307; Turner, *Matthew*, 231) refer to Lev 5:3 but do not explain the distinction between contracting ritual impurity and transgressing a commandment of the Lord.

107. Milgrom, *Leviticus*, 307.

108. Jesus' undergoing ritual purification should not be any more confusing than his undergoing baptism, which the Gospels attest (Matt 3:13–17; Mark 1:9–11; Luke 3:21–22) and which Jesus describes as necessary so that he might "fulfill all righteousness" (Matt 3:15). Nor should those (including myself) who believe that Jesus confronted the temple system and predicted its destruction (e.g., Matt 24:1–4) find Jesus' upholding laws of ritual purification confusing. Jesus predicted the destruction of the temple in the future, which leaves the temple system intact (however corrupt it may or may not have been) until its destruction. Given that the temple was still standing during the ministry of Jesus, he would naturally have expected the ritual cleansing required in the law to be performed *until the destruction of the temple*. Further on this, see the Appendix "Thoughts on Jesus, Paul and the Law."

109. See Crossley, *Date*, 83—except that Crossley refers to the Marcan parallel.

(or both). Jesus observed the commandment about wearing tassels as part of his obedience to God his Father.

In a wonderful (if at first slightly odd) little story, we see another aspect of Jesus' commitment to the law (Matt 17:24–27). Collectors of the temple tax approached Peter to ask if Jesus paid this tax. The law required that every Israelite paid half a shekel yearly for the service of the tabernacle (Exod 30:11–16).[110] At the time of Jesus, this tax paid for the sacrificial system in the Jerusalem temple (Josephus, *Ant.* 18.312).[111] Peter replied that Jesus did pay this tax. When they were inside the house, Jesus asked Peter whether earthly kings charge their children or other people tax. Peter made the obvious reply that they charged others, and then Jesus pointed out that the sons are therefore free from taxation. The implication must be that Jesus, as Son of God, has no need to pay the temple tax.[112] Nonetheless,

---

110. There has been some dispute about whether this was the temple tax of Exod 30:11–16 or a Roman tax. For a defense of reading this as the temple tax, see Davies and Allison, *Matthew*, 2:739–41.

111. Harrington, *Matthew*, 261–62; Davies and Allison, *Matthew*, 2:743.

112. Harrington, *Matthew*, 261–62. In support of this reading it ought to be noted that Matthew makes Jesus as Son of God a dominant theme in his gospel: see e.g., Kingsbury, *Christology*; Kingsbury, *Story*; Davies and Allison, *Matthew*, 1:339; Harrington, *Matthew*, 18; Luz, *Matthew 1–7*, 144. Therefore, the audience of his gospel will naturally think of the Son of God who is free from taxation as Jesus. Moreover, the question of the tax collectors was whether Jesus paid the tax—not whether anyone else should pay the tax—so it makes most sense to assume that his words respond to the issue of whether *he* should pay the tax. We have no need to read the plural language of the parable ("from their sons" and "the sons are free," vv. 25–26) into the interpretation and application of the parable to the question of whether Jesus as Son of God should pay the tax. Therefore, the idea that we should read either all the sons of Israel (e.g., Davies and Allison, *Matthew*, 2:745) or all the Christians (e.g., Hagner, *Matthew 14–28*, 512) into "the sons" of vv. 25–26 ought to be rejected. Given that the story relates to the temple and the temple tax, attempts to read the story as really being a vehicle for exploring a theological point unrelated to the temple or temple tax, relating to a period not indicated in the text and a situation between Christians and Jews not indicated in the text (e.g., Nolland, *Matthew*, 726–27), are unnecessary. After the fall of the temple in AD 70, Vespasian continued the collection of the tax but used it for the temple of Jupiter Capitolinus in Rome (Josephus, *J.W.* 7.218). Were Matthew to have developed this story for a situation after the fall of the Jerusalem temple, he probably would have excised the saying of Jesus "but so as not to scandalize anyone" (Matt 17:27) as surely little could have been more scandalous than the Son of the one true God of the Jews choosing to support idolatry on the basis that he did not want to cause a stir. So, we do better to interpret the text as concerning the temple and temple tax relating to the period in which the temple was still standing.

Jesus tells Peter what he must do to find the necessary money to go and pay the tax. He obeys the law.[113]

On another occasion, a young man approached Jesus to ask what good thing or things he must do to inherit eternal life (Matt 19:16–22). Jesus responded: "if you wish to enter life, keep the commandments" (Matt 19:17b). When the man asked which ones, Jesus specified the commands against murder, adultery, stealing, and bearing false witness, as well as the commands to honor father and mother, and love your neighbor as yourself (Exod 20:12–16; Lev 19:18; Deut 5:16–20). Jesus not only upheld the law but taught the law. When he went on to instruct the young man to sell his possessions and give the proceeds to the poor, his instruction was fully in line with the commandments in the law to help the poor (e.g., Deut 15:11).

A lawyer once approached Jesus to quiz him on the Torah (Matt 22:34–40). He asked "which is the greatest commandment in the law?" (Matt 22:36). Jesus replied that to love the Lord your God with all your heart, soul, and understanding was the greatest commandment—citing Deut 6:5. He added that there was another like it, to love your neighbor as yourself—quoting Lev 19:18. Jesus drew from the law the two greatest commandments in the law, and claimed that the whole law and the prophets hung on these two commandments (Matt 22:40). He did not replace the law with these two commandments or use them to determine which laws might be dropped or retained. Instead, he pointed out that these two laws showed what the whole of the law was about.[114] For Jesus, love was the heart of the law and this was clear from the love commandments, which were part of the law.

So, it is deeply ironic that those who promote the comforting myth that Jesus taught that love replaced the law tend to draw on sayings such as this one to make their point. Far from proving that Jesus replaced the law with love, this saying demonstrates that the Jesus who taught love of God and neighbor was fully committed to the law. Not only that, but the reason

---

113. This wonderful story opens up all sorts of questions about Jesus and his relationship to the temple—not least as he predicts its destruction in Matt 24:1–2. Proper treatment of such questions requires more than a footnote. Suffice it to say that there is no contradiction in Jesus (a) believing the temple was central in the life of his disciples until its destruction and (b) predicting its destruction. This makes sense both of his prediction of the temple's destruction and of his upholding its institutions (e.g., sending the leper to the priest [Matt 8:4]). It also makes sense of the Lucan witness to both the early Christians worshipping in the temple (Luke 24:53) and their speaking against it (Acts 6:13).

114. Davies and Allison, *Matthew*, 3:245–46.

The Jesus *Really* Didn't Know

he was committed to loving God and neighbor was precisely because it was found in the law. Jesus taught that people should love God and each other because the law commanded it.

In a tirade against Pharisees, in which Jesus criticizes a number of their practices, he comments on the topic of tithing (Matt 23:23). The law commands tithing of all produce of the land (Lev 27:30; Deut 14:22). Although it does not specify herbs, it is reasonably easy to understand how the command to tithe all produce from the land might be understood to include herbs such as mint, dill, and cumin (as some rabbis did).[115] Jesus does not question the importance of tithing all produce. He says that it is necessary to do this as well as paying proper attention to matters of justice, mercy, and faith (or faithfulness). Jesus upholds the law here beyond the requirements of at least some later Pharisees, who did not see tithing herbs as necessary to fulfill the law (m. Ma'aś 4:5).[116] So, Jesus did uphold and obey the law.

Despite popular myths to the contrary, in his own actions Jesus did not break the law. Nor did he teach others to break the law. Quite the opposite is true, Jesus taught people to keep God's commandments. The comforting myths that we have told ourselves—that God came in Jesus to show us his love and free us from the obligations of obeying God's commands—are simply untrue. Not only did Jesus not break the law, but Jesus obeyed the law. If by the word "legalist" we mean someone who takes God's commandments seriously, thinks that they should be obeyed, and teaches others to obey them, then Jesus was more of a "legalist" than the Pharisees.[117]

---

115. Rabbi Eliezer taught that dill was subject to the law of tithes but other rabbis disagreed, stating that amongst herbs only cress and rocket were (m. Ma'aś 4:5). The Mishnah also requires the tithing of cumin (m. Demai 2:1). Given these texts, there ought to be little difficulty in assuming that Jesus and Matthew were aware of a Pharisaic tradition that taught tithing mint, dill, and cumin. Given these texts, this tradition was probably also a matter of dispute amongst the rabbis.

116. Some would argue that Matt 24:20 ("pray that your flight should not be in winter or on a Sabbath") also suggests that the Matthean Jesus is sensitive to Sabbath law (e.g., Crossley, *Date*, 105). I am not convinced. The Torah does not state how far one may travel on the Sabbath and given the teaching of Jesus not to set up human traditions against the command of God, it would seem odd for the Matthean Jesus to suddenly teach the necessity of having scruples about rabbinic traditions over the need to flee for their lives. Given the difficulty of travelling in winter, I assume that Jesus also thinks that travel must be somehow difficult on the Sabbath.

117. If by the word "legalist" we mean someone who thinks they can earn their salvation through good works, then Jesus is not a legalist because he clearly called people to repent to receive God's forgiveness and then live in obedience. By the same token, nor

Jesus does not teach the replacement of the commandments in the law with the idea that we should simply do "the loving thing" whether it fits God's instructions or not. Jesus does not teach love of God and neighbor as some kind of stand-alone love ethic, but he teaches them because the law commands love of God and neighbor. He does not teach these commandments as a replacement of the law but precisely as commandments in the law. He sees no contradiction between love and the law. Rather, the law hangs together precisely as an outworking of loving God and neighbor. Jesus does disagree with the Pharisees but not because he wants to break the law for the sake of some love ethic. He criticizes the Pharisees because they broke the law to make life more manageable for themselves rather than obeying God's commandments as set out in the law (e.g., Matt 15:3–9). Jesus demands that they obey God's commands instead of their own interpretations of his commands. Jesus did not teach them love instead of law. He taught the Pharisees to love God by obeying his commandments rather than loving themselves by making his commands easier to obey or even non-obligatory. Jesus also disagreed with them on some interpretation of the law and how God called people to live in obedience to it. Even so, a Torah-observing ("legalistic") Pharisee could not but completely agree with Jesus on the importance of love of God and neighbor because Jesus drew these commandments straight from the law.

Jesus teaches obedience to God's commands because he wants people to enter the kingdom of heaven.[118] He knows that people sin and need forgiveness. He offers people forgiveness through repentance, which involves changing the way we live and leading lives of obedience to God. Jesus teaches that his interpretation of the law is final. People find the true interpretation of God's commands only in his teaching. Therefore, to obey the commandments of God we have to live out the teaching of Jesus. Jesus described those who listen to and live out his teaching as wise. He identified those who listen to but do not live out his teaching as foolish. The wise reap

---

were many of his Jewish contemporaries legalists, as they believed that they had been saved (from Egypt) by the grace and power of God, and that they were kept in relationship with God only through his grace and forgiveness of their sins. That is why they performed sin offerings in the temple and carried out the prescribed rituals on the Day of Atonement each year (Leviticus 16).

118. Presumably, this is why his ministry opens in Matthew and Mark with the command "repent for the kingdom of heaven is at hand" (Matt 4:17; cf. Mark 1:14–15). God will judge and only those who are judged righteous will enjoy the eternal kingdom—for which righteousness we need God's forgiveness.

the reward of the kingdom of heaven while the foolish reap destruction. The answer to judgment is to repent of our sins and then learn to live out the teaching of Jesus.

This Jesus can seem more challenging than the Jesus of some contemporary popular imaginations: the Jesus who forgives us endlessly, indulges our peccadillos, and promises us his blessing both now and hereafter—without asking anything in return. In fact, some can find the Jesus of the gospel rather unattractive when compared with this figure of contemporary religious fantasy. However, the truth is rather different. Jesus requires something of us. Or, more correctly, Jesus requires *everything* of us. In his words (Matt 16:24–27):

> If anyone wants to come after me, let them deny themselves and take up their cross and let them follow me. 25 For whoever wants to save their life will lose it; whoever loses their life on account of me will find it. 26 For what does it benefit anyone if they gain the whole world but lose their life? What will somebody give in exchange for their life? 27 For the Son of Man is going to come in the glory of his Father with his angels, and then he will repay each person according to their actions.

Jesus wants people to give their lives over entirely to following him, and this involves obedience to his teachings. Such obedience stands them in good stead on the day when he comes as Son of Man to judge every human being according to what they have done. Clearly Jesus believes that forgiveness clears sins, but he expects obedience to follow repentance. A story he once told makes this perfectly clear (Matt 21:28–31a):

> What do you think? A man had two sons. And going up to the first, he said, "Son, go today and work in the vineyard." 29 But he replied, "I don't want to." Later on, he changed his mind and went. 30 And going to the other [son] he said the same thing. And this one said, "Right away, sir." And he did not go. 31 Which of the two did the will of the Father?

The answer is obvious: the first one. He may have rebelled initially but he changed his mind—he had regrets about his initial decision and acted differently. In the context of this story, Jesus talks about tax collectors and prostitutes (who had clearly regretted their actions and turned to follow Jesus) entering the kingdom of God (Matt 21:31).[119] Jesus believes that re-

---

119. Contextually, it makes no sense to assume that they had not changed their behavior. If they were still practicing extortion and selling sex, then this would not show the

pentant sinners are forgiven their sins. However, he equally believes that repentant sinners change their ways—they actually regret doing wrong and seek to live differently, following Jesus' commands. The Jesus of the Gospels does not want his disciples to live lawlessly but to follow up their repentance of their sins with living in obedience to his commands. And this Jesus, the real Jesus, may be someone we do not particularly want to know. But where we may hide from this Jesus—or paper over his face with pictures of other Jesuses we prefer—it may be because we have never really understood him. Perhaps even, we never knew him. But that does not change Jesus' offer to any of us. He stands at the door and knocks, waiting for us to answer (Rev 3:20). He longs to reprove and discipline us because he loves us (Rev 3:19). He invites us, as teacher, to come and learn from him—an invitation to which we now turn, as in it we find Jesus' answer to judgment.

---

repentance the first son did. Jesus compares these repentant tax collectors and prostitutes who have changed their ways and follow Jesus' teaching to the chief priests and elders of the people who like the first son have said they are willing but do not follow Jesus' teaching.

4

The Jesus You Didn't Know—*Really?*

We are not alone. Faced with some of the basic truths about the real Jesus, the one the Gospel stories tell us about, we might feel differently. Jesus preaches judgment. At the end of time, Jesus, the Son of Man, will sit on his heavenly throne, judge all people, and repay every single one of us according to our actions here on earth (Matt 16:27). He will judge justly, and that means that our sins count against us. He will forgive us if we repent. However, he expects us to truly repent and so follow up our saying sorry by changing our behavior. He does not teach us that the love of God means we can forget all about obedience to God's commands. He expects us to be obedient to God's commands. The greater part of his ministry here on earth was spent teaching us what obedience to God's commands looks like and instructing us to live like this. For any of us who have been told, and believed, the comforting myths that Jesus came to replace "legalism" with "love," the Jesus of the Gospel stories may come across as really rather challenging. Faced with this Jesus, we may feel cut loose from the God we want to worship. But we are not alone. In fact, we are anything but alone.

A teaching presence

Jesus himself tells us that we are not alone (Matt 28:18–20).

> And the eleven disciples went to Galilee to the mountain which Jesus had commanded them to go to, 17 and seeing him they worshipped him although some doubted. 18 And coming towards them Jesus spoke to them, "all authority in heaven and on earth has been given to me. 19 Therefore go, make disciples of all the nations: baptizing them into the name of the Father, and the Son and the Holy Spirit; 20 teaching them to obey all the things I have commanded you and look, I will be with you every day until the end of the age."

Jesus makes a promise to be present with his disciples every day until the end of the age, the time when he comes again as Son of Man to judge all people (Matt 13:40–42, 49–50). However, this is no vague promise of a comforting presence. Jesus links this promise to what he says before with the words "and look." This link signals that Jesus' promise has something to do with what he was talking about in the words immediately preceding this promise.

The context of the promise is Jesus' "great commission"—his instruction to his disciples to make disciples of all the nations of the world.[1] The basic instruction is "go, make disciples." There are two activities that making disciples involves: baptizing and teaching.[2] Baptism by washing or bathing in water involves repentance (Matt 3:7, 11). This is why those who came to be baptized by John the Baptist in the Gospel stories confessed their sins (Matt 3:6). Baptism also involves the outpouring of the Holy Spirit on those who have confessed their sins (Matt 3:11).[3] So the first part of

---

1. Or possibly "all the gentile nations." For "all the nations of the world," see France, *Matthew*, 1114–15. For "all the Gentiles," see Harrington, *Matthew*, 414–15. For the argument in this book, nothing hangs on which way we translate this verb, so I will simply leave the readers of this footnote checking out these commentary references and the articles to which they point. Personally, I am still more persuaded by the evidence Harrington presents.

2. The grammar of the Greek text makes this perfectly clear. The aorist imperative "make disciples" (*mathēteusate*) carries two dependent present participles, "baptizing" (*baptidzontes*) and "teaching" (*didaskontes*). The fact that these participles are dependent on the main verb "make disciples" demonstrates that they are simply the two aspects of the activity of making disciples that Jesus instructs his disciples to go and do.

3. I am well aware that the Greek might be translated "he will baptize you in holy spirit and fire," without a capital H or S on holy spirit. However, given the connection to Matt 28:19, where baptism is in the name of *the* Father, *the* Son, and *the* Holy Spirit, it occurs to me that Matthew saw the Holy Spirit as at least as personal as the Father and the Son. Hence, I translate the Holy Spirit in Matt 3:11 also. I see no reason to presuppose that Matthew changed his understanding of the Holy Spirit during the course of writing

making disciples involves their confession of their sins and turning around to lead a new and holy life following the commandments of God, and their being filled with the Holy Spirit. The second part of disciple making is teaching and it involves exactly what Jesus instructs here: teaching the nations "to obey all the things which I have commanded you" (Matt 28:20a). Discipleship involves not only repentance (confessing sins, receiving forgiveness and turning from sin) but learning to live out in practice all of Jesus' commands. Learning to live out his teachings prepares people for the end of the age when as Son of Man he comes to judge all.

It is in the context of this mission that Jesus makes his promise to be with the disciples. As they go out into all the nations of the world to make other disciples of the people they meet, baptizing them as they repent of their sins, and teaching them to live out Jesus' commands in their daily lives, Jesus promises to be with them. He commits himself to being with his disciples in this mission work "every day." However, this promise ought not to be read as primarily or even basically a commitment to be present with his disciples when *they are at work* in mission. Reading his promise with his earlier teaching in Matt 23:8, his promise can only really be understood as *his commitment to be at work amongst his disciples* as they go out in mission.

The Jesus who promises to be with his disciples has already taught them that he is the only teacher: "You are not to be called 'rabbi' because you have one teacher and you are all disciples" (Matt 23:8). Reading Jesus' great commission in the light of this earlier statement, we have to conclude that the disciples may be teaching but they are not the teacher. *Jesus* is the teacher.[4] Therefore, as they go out to baptize and teach, they are working

---

his gospel, or that he was somehow subtly indicating that John the Baptist held a radically different pneumatology from Jesus. I am also aware that the general understanding is that fully developed trinitarian doctrine only appears in later centuries and so is not present in Matthew (Davies and Allison, *Matthew*, 3:686). This is fair enough. The debates about the Trinity only occurred in later centuries. However, this does not mean that Matthew did not hold some kind of understanding of God in the persons of Father, Son, and Holy Spirit. The Didache uses exactly the same words as Matthew "in the name of the Father, the Son, and the Holy Spirit" as a baptismal formula (Did. 7:1). As the Didache has formularized the phrase by AD 100, it seems reasonable to me to assume that Matthew may have used it similarly—particularly if he wrote his gospel in the second half of the first century, as many assume. For this date for the Didache, see the discussion of Bart D. Ehrman (in *The Apostolic Fathers*, 411).

4. Either there is a glaring contradiction between Jesus' self-identification in Matt 23:8 and his commission to his disciples in Matt 28:18–20, or Matthew intends these verses to be read together. It is also possible that Matthew has Jesus change his mind (for whatever reason) over whether or not he is the only teacher really between chapters 23

with, in, and through the one great teacher, who exercises his teaching ministry amongst, through, and alongside his disciples. His promise of presence among them is actually a commitment to be ministering in, through, and alongside them as they engage in ministry. These words of promise are Jesus' commitment to be a teaching presence amongst his disciples.

Similarly, reading these two texts together has something to say about the role to which Jesus calls his disciples. He has called them to make disciples of all nations. They are to baptize all those who come to faith in the name of the Father, Son, and Holy Spirit. They are to teach all those who commit to following Jesus to obey everything he commanded them. However, they do not do this as teachers but as disciples themselves: "You are not to be called 'rabbi' because you have one teacher and *you are all disciples*." (Matt 23:8). Those who go out in ministry and mission go out as continuing disciples of the one true teacher. They are not and do not become teachers. There is only one teacher. They remain disciples as they minister.[5]

Something else follows on from this. Disciples who go out in mission make fellow disciples of Jesus. They do not convert people who then become their own students or disciples. Jesus remains the one true teacher who is present amongst his disciples as a teaching presence as they engage in the ministry of teaching others to obey his commands. In this ministry, the disciples are not to be called or think of themselves as teachers, but as disciples. So, as disciples they continue to learn from Jesus himself to obey all that he has commanded at the same time as they share in Jesus' teaching ministry helping other disciples to learn to obey his commands. In their mission to the nations, the disciples remain followers of Jesus, learning obedience to his teaching as they engage in the ministry of teaching others to do the same.

This ministry clearly calls for humility. Jesus may not specify this in his great commission (Matt 28:18–20) but he does earlier in the Gospel story (Matt 7:1–5):

---

and 28 of his gospel. But Matthew does not indicate this change of mind in any way. So, I take the text of Matthew as it stands, and assume that the character and teaching of Jesus is best read as consistent, at least at first, and interpret the text appropriately.

5. Some readers of this book involved in teaching ministry have asked what this means in practice—not least for those of us involved in teaching ministry (and especially as Paul names "teachers" as a class of minister, Eph 4:11). Read on and by the end of chapter 4 the picture ought to be clearer. Basically, teachers in the church only participate in the teaching ministry of Jesus and so teach only his teaching and what is in line with his teaching. More to the point, they only do so with the humility of one who is still first and foremost a disciple.

> Do not judge, so that you may not be judged. 2 For by the judgment you use to judge others you yourself will be judged, and with the measure you measure out, it will be measured out for you. 3 And why are you looking at the splinter in your fellow disciple's eye, but fail to even notice the wooden beam in your own eye? 4 How on earth can you say to your fellow disciple, "let me take the splinter out of your eye," when there is a whacking great big wooden beam in your own eye? 5 You hypocrite, first take the beam out of your own eye and then you will be able to see clearly enough to take the splinter out of your fellow disciple's eye.[6]

Jesus is talking to his disciples here (Matt 5:1). He explains to his disciples how they are to treat each other. The comical picture of a disciple with a wooden beam in their eye trying to get a splinter out of their fellow disciple's eye is not designed to prevent disciples from helping each other to obey Jesus' commands. Quite the opposite is true. Jesus ends the picture with the instruction to take the beam out, to see clearly so that they can take the splinter out of their fellow disciple's eye. This is an image through which Jesus teaches his disciples how they are to help each other grow in obedience to his commands. Disciples are to sort out their own problems before they try to tackle the same problems in and with other disciples. The image of the splinter and the wooden beam is quite deliberate.[7] A splinter is a small part of a beam. So, the disciple trying to help their fellow disciple become more obedient to Jesus actually has the same moral difficulty but has it in far greater measure. Disciples who are trying to help other disciples become more obedient to Jesus should do so as those who have a realistic understanding of their own character and moral behavior, and they should only help others to grow in obedience to Jesus' teaching in areas in which they are growing in obedience themselves.

---

6. This translation is not quite as literal as others elsewhere in the book. A literal translation simply does not get the force of the statement (and so fails to translate the meaning). For example, the literal translation, "or how will you say to your brother, 'allow [me], I will cast out the splinter from your eye,' and behold the beam in your own eye" does not really capture the force of the statement as well as the freer translation "how on earth can you say to your fellow disciple, 'let me take the splinter out of your eye,' when there is a whacking great big wooden beam in your own eye?'" I freely admit there are no words for "whacking great big" in the Greek text. I use them to capture the force of the statement so that the translation does not render Jesus' statement stilted, "worthy" and quaint.

7. For an explanation of "splinter" and "wooden beam" as the better translations (against e.g., "speck" or "mote"), see Davies and Allison, *Matthew*, 1:671.

Jesus issues a warning with this call to humility. Those disciples who judge their fellow disciples, particularly when they themselves struggle with the same moral difficulty, will be judged by God at the final judgment (Matt 7:1).[8] Jesus does not tolerate moral hypocrisy in the teaching ministry of his disciples. The early Christians knew this well. James comments: "Do not let many become teachers, my fellow disciples, seeing that we (teachers) will receive a stricter judgment" (Jas 3:1).[9] Those set apart for a ministry that was focused on teaching Jesus' commands and enabling others to obey them will be judged more strictly.

But this is positive. The teaching ministry in which Jesus promises to be present is one marked by the humility of those coming alongside their fellow disciples to teach them obedience. They do this as disciples who are also learning obedience from the one true teacher. All Christians learn together from the one true teacher. As Jesus put it earlier in the Gospel: "but you are all disciples" (Matt 23:8). The word translated "disciples" is the word for "brothers and sisters." This draws on an image of an ideal family with functioning bonds of love between siblings. Jesus uses language that demonstrates that he envisages his disciples learning together from him and teaching each other in love and lifelong commitment towards one another. The warning of judgment makes it clear that Jesus commits himself as a teaching presence amongst his disciples to growing them together in humility and love towards each other as they grow in obedience to his commands. This is precisely how Jesus himself commits to teaching his disciples obedience to his commands.

The nature of the teacher

Later in the Gospel, Jesus says as much (Matt 11:28–30).

> Come to me all who are exhausted and heavily burdened, and I will give you rest. 29 Take my yoke upon yourselves and learn from me, because I am meek and humble in heart and mind. And

---

8. I read Matt 7:3–5 as continuing the thought of Matt 7:1–2 as v. 3 demonstrates that it continues the thought of vv. 1–2 by the use of the conjunction *de* ("and").

9. Whether you read James as first century (e.g., Johnson, *James*, 92–121) or early second century (e.g., Dibelius, *James*, 11–21; Allison, *James*, 3–32) makes little difference here. This is still early Christianity. Personally, I am more convinced by Johnson's arguments for an early dating of James.

you will find rest for your souls. 30 For my yoke is fitting and my burden is light.

In these words, Jesus promises rest to those who are weighed down by trying to obey God, following the teachings and interpretations of the law offered by other rabbis. He offers them rest if they follow his (final and ultimate) interpretation of the law, and if they learn to obey his commands by learning from him.

This saying makes little sense and feels rather cruel if interpreted as an invitation to rest from the troubles of life, as commonly happens in Christian talks and sermons.[10] It makes little sense because the promise of rest is quite enough for those who are shattered by the turmoil that life can bring. There is no need for people to take anything more upon themselves or learn anything in particular, if all Jesus means to offer is rest for the exhausted. It feels cruel because if people are weighed down or crushed under too many burdens in life, what kind of religious teacher (or God) would tell them to take on more? In this situation, the instruction "take my yoke upon you" seems like mockery of those who are already overburdened. This popular reading of the text, however, seems to be mistaken. Reading the text with some historical details in mind makes much better sense of these verses.

The term "yoke" was a metaphor used by rabbis to talk about the law.[11] Rabbi Nehunya ben Haqqaneh used the word this way when he stated that those who do not immerse themselves in the Torah will end up suffering political oppression (m. 'Abot 3:5).[12]

> From whoever accepts upon himself the yoke of the Torah do they remove the yoke of the state and the yoke of hard labor. And upon whoever removes from himself the yoke of the Torah do they lay the yoke of the state and the yoke of hard labor.

The term "yoke" was used to refer to the law in the Old Testament (Jer 5:5) and also in early Christian writings (Acts 15:10; Gal 5:1).

---

10. France (*Matthew*, 448) entertains the possibility that "they may be metaphors for the difficulties and pressures of life in general" before focusing on the more usual scholarly interpretation.

11. Davies and Allison, *Matthew*, 2:289.

12. Rabbi Nehunya ben Haqqaneh belonged to the first generation of the Tannaim, and so his use of "yoke" to refer to the Torah demonstrates that the term was used this way by rabbis at the time of Jesus.

The word "burden" refers to interpretations of the law.[13] Jesus criticizes the Pharisees for "tying up burdens that are heavy and hard to bear, and they place them on people's shoulders, and they themselves do not wish to lift a finger to move them" (Matt 23:4). Placing these burdens on people's shoulders makes them sound like yokes.[14] The burdens that the Pharisees placed on the shoulders of others in practice were their interpretations of the Torah. Given that the word "yoke" might refer to the law and that within the Gospel the term "burden" seems to refer to the Pharisees interpretations of the Torah, it seems sensible to interpret this saying of Jesus with this historical context in mind.

The people whom Jesus invites into rest are those who are heavily burdened. They are the people who are trying to carry the burden of the Pharisees' interpretations of the Torah. Their efforts have weighed them down, they are "heavily burdened." They have become exhausted in their efforts to try to live righteous and holy lives in the ways that the Pharisees have been teaching them. Jesus promises them rest. He tells them that they will find rest for their souls if they take his yoke upon themselves and learn from him.

Interestingly, no Jewish rabbi ever told another to take up their yoke of the Torah. Nor has any reference to the "yoke of Moses" been identified in any ancient text.[15] So, when Jesus uses the phrase "my yoke" he says something very out of the ordinary because it suggests that the law to which he refers is his own. Given his presentation of himself, later in the Gospel, as the one true rabbi who gives the ultimate interpretation of the law, his words "my yoke" must refer to his own final interpretation of the law. Given that he says "my yoke" rather than "my thoughts about or interpretation of the yoke of the law," he must think that his interpretation of the law is in fact now "the law." This makes sense of why he follows his instruction "take my yoke upon yourselves" with the invitation "and learn from me." If the "yoke" is his interpretation of the law (which from now on *is* the law), then it is appropriate that his disciples learn from him—as disciples learn the law and obedience to the law from their teachers.

Jesus gives a reason for learning from him (as opposed to any other rabbi). He criticizes the Pharisees for interpreting the law in ways that give

---

13. Hagner, *Matthew 1–13*, 324–25; Gundry, *Matthew*, 219; Luz, *Matthew 8–20*, 172; France, *Matthew*, 448.

14. Davies and Allison, *Matthew*, 2:271.

15. Davies and Allison, *Matthew*, 2:291–92.

people intolerably heavy burdens under which they labor with absolutely no help from the Pharisees themselves (Matt 23:4). By contrast, Jesus promises to be a meek teacher. Meekness combines humility with strength. It is mild and gentle friendliness, but not spinelessness or weakness. The meek leader exercises gentleness in judgment, combining this with wisdom and kindness.[16] As teacher, Jesus approaches his disciples in humility and gentleness. Jesus also promises to be "humble in heart and mind." Literally, Jesus' words would be translated "humble in heart."[17] However, the heart in Jewish thinking was the seat of the emotions and the mind, and particularly of the will.[18] So, when Jesus describes himself as humble in heart and mind, he means that he comes alongside his disciples as he teaches them rather than talking down at them. He teaches his disciples obedience to his commands as one who comes alongside them in gentleness, humility, and kindness. Jesus is not so much a purpose-driven trainer as a person-centered teacher and pastor.

This is why Jesus promises that people can find rest for their souls in him. His teachings may be strict (indeed, some of them stricter than those of some of the Pharisees) but he is not an oppressive moral overlord. He does not issue commands and then tell people to get on with them without offering the slightest help to put them into practice. He promises to come alongside those who come to him, and he comes alongside them in gentleness, humility, and kindness. He teaches us obedience to his commands, knowing our frailty and weakness. He does not condemn us for this but sticks with us throughout the learning process, gently and kindly enabling us to learn. The process of learning obedience with him is marked by love, kindness, gentleness, and understanding. Jesus' disciples can trust him to

---

16. Hauck and Schulz, "πραΰς, πραΰτης," *TDNT* 6:645–46. Having offered a summary of the classical background to this word in these pages, they suggest that in the Gospel of Matthew the term refers to weakness. Davies and Allison (*Matthew*, 1:449) similarly suggest it means powerless. In the Gospel of Matthew, Jesus presents himself as the only true teacher of the Torah, who presents the final interpretation of the Torah. In Matt 11:28–30, he invites people to come to him in this role. His very words *"my* Torah" suggest that he sees himself as greater than Moses, even on a par with God the Father, who was the first lawgiver. He does not give the impression that he sees himself as weak in the area of lawgiving or teaching the law. Rather, he sees himself as above Moses (Davies and Allison, *Matthew*, 2:290). In this context, it is remarkably hard to read Jesus as suggesting that he is weak. Meekness, with its sense of genuine gentleness in one more powerful, seems to fit the context much better.

17. The Greek *tapeinos tē kardia* literally translates as "humble in heart."

18. Behm, "καρδία," *TDNT* 3:611–12.

help them to learn, and that is why they can finally lay their moral burdens down and rest in him.

His disciples can trust him precisely because he will not leave them. We are not alone in the process of learning how to live out his teachings. Literally, when Jesus promises to be with his disciples "every day" until the end of the age, he commits to coming alongside us "all day every day" (Matt 28:20).[19] The promise of Jesus' teaching presence amongst us is for as long as this world lasts. Jesus will not abandon his disciples. He will not even leave them for one moment. He is with us constantly, ready to teach each one of us his ways in gentleness and love.

Jesus' fulfilment of the law

This brings us back to one of the more difficult sayings of Jesus (Matt 5:17):

> Do not say to yourselves that I have come to destroy the law or the prophets: I have not come to destroy them but to fulfill them.

Jesus certainly does not want to abolish or annul the law. However, neither does he want to replace the law with a morally anemic "love" that has no boundaries and becomes an excuse for people to ignore their wrongdoing and continue in it under the (mistaken) impression that God has it all covered and does not really mind. (For the mistakenness of this impression, re-read Matt 7:21–23). During the course of the Gospel story, Jesus offers his final interpretation of the law. Some of his commands seem remarkably stringent and difficult to obey. Nevertheless, his words in Matt 5:17 ought not to be read as ferocious words of threatening "legalism" because love lies at the heart of these words.

In this statement, *Jesus himself* fulfills the law (and the prophets) *by teaching us*, his disciples, obedience to his commands. Although he calls his disciples to follow him, to come to him and to learn from him, he puts the onus on himself to fulfill the law: "*I* have come . . . to fulfill." He fulfills the law through his teaching ministry. He invites us to take *his* yoke upon ourselves—that is, to learn his interpretation of the law (which is now the law). He invites us to learn from him because he will teach each one of us in gentleness and humility how to live out his commands. This is probably why Matthew puts this saying about his fulfilling the law near the beginning of

---

19. Charlie Moule (*Idiom Book*, 34) comments on the accusative *pasa tas hēmeras* "perhaps strictly = *the whole of every day*."

the Sermon on the Mount, right at the start of Jesus' ministry. Those reading the Gospel story can then read how Jesus fulfills the law in his teaching ministry, in his death and resurrection, and then in his continuing teaching ministry present amongst his disciples as they go out in mission to make disciples of all the nations.

And Jesus fulfills the law as a particular kind of teacher. He comes alongside his disciples to teach them in humility, gentleness, and love. He does not stand over us as a threatening moral overlord. He offers rest for weary hearts and minds by teaching us in humility and compassion how to live according to God's ways. In doing so, he mends sinful and broken lives. He remains committed to teaching each and every one of his disciples in kindness and humility all day every day until the end of the age. Jesus lifts more than a finger to help us live out his teachings.

A Pauline question mark?

But what about Paul? There may well be some readers who are asking where their Pauline gospel has gone. Surely Christ died for our sins and we are now forgiven by him? On the cross, Jesus paid the price for our sins. Jesus' death on the cross defeated sin. God put him forward as an atoning sacrifice or propitiation to avert his wrath. Jesus has taken upon himself the judgment we deserve. He died on our behalf. We are now reconciled to God. Why all this talk of Jesus coming to teach us how to live? Surely the point of the gospel is that we no longer need to worry about living according to the law precisely because Christ has died for our sins. We are forgiven. Does not this talk of obedience to Jesus' commands simply set up a new law? Was not that the problem of the Galatian church? Talking about obedience to God's or Jesus' commands just sets up a new law. Paul's ministry was all about preventing that kind of new law being set up, surely?

Not quite. Actually, all this talk of obedience to Jesus' teaching fits Paul rather well. Paul did believe that God put Jesus forward as an atoning sacrifice or propitiation for our sins, and that this free gift of grace makes us righteous (Rom 3:24–25).[20] He did believe that Jesus Christ died on our

---

20. I realize that the Greek term *hilastērion* (translated here as "atoning sacrifice" or "propitiation") has occasioned much discussion. For solid discussions of the issue, see Fitzmyer (*Romans*, 349–50) and Moo (*Romans*, 231–43). I would nuance their discussions with the observation that if the wrath of God is the problem (which it is according to Paul in Rom 1:18), then the answer must be something that sorts out the wrath of God. The propitiation of the anger of God (if *hilastērion* is to be read as "propitiation,"

behalf (1 Thess 5:9–10). He stated quite clearly that having been made righteous, we have peace with God through our Lord Jesus Christ (Rom 5:1). Paul also proclaimed that there is no condemnation for those who are in Christ Jesus (Rom 8:1). But Paul did not stop there. He warned the Christians in Rome about the consequences of taking Christ for granted (Rom 11:22): "so, take note of the generosity and severity of God: severity on those who have fallen, but generosity upon you yourself, if you remain in [his] generosity—otherwise you yourself will be cut off too." The Paul who stated that there is no condemnation for those who are in Christ Jesus also warned Christian disciples to remain within the generosity of God. The context of the statement is quite clear: a warning to gentile Christians not to get all high and mighty about their new status in Christ (Rom 11:13–25a). Remaining in God's generosity is not only continuing to seek forgiveness but also continuing to show love and openness to others receiving the gospel.

However, remaining in the generosity of God involves more than showing love to those outside the faith or who have fallen away from faith in God. Paul wanted to prepare his fellow disciples for the day on which Christ would come again to judge. Paul litters his letters with encouragements to them and his fellow ministers to live holy lives in view of this fact that Christ would come again to judge all people: "for our salvation is closer than when we first believed . . . so let us put away the works of darkness" (Rom 13:11–12); "or do you not know that wrongdoers will not inherit the kingdom of God?" (1 Cor 6:9); "as a result, we make it our ambition (whether at home or away) to be well-pleasing to him, for it is necessary for all of us to appear before the judgment seat of Christ for each of us to receive our just deserts for what we did while alive, whether good or worthless" (2 Cor 5:9–10); "now the works of the flesh are clear enough . . . I warn you, just as I have warned you, that those who do things like this will not inherit the kingdom of God" (Gal 5:19–21); "do not even mention sexual immorality, any uncleanness, or greed to each other; . . . know this, that no sexually immoral person, or unclean person, or greedy person (they are idolaters) will have an inheritance in the kingdom of Christ and of God" (Eph 5:3–5); "become fellow imitators of me, brothers and

---

even as one meaning amongst others) in Rom 3:25 seems to be the only place in Romans where Paul talks of anything that might avert the wrath of God. If his anger has not been dealt with here then we arrive at the end of Romans with the wrath of God fully in place and directed towards every impiety and unrighteousness—which is not good news for humanity.

sisters, and watch closely those who live out the example they have in us, for many live as enemies to the cross of Christ, . . . their end is destruction" (Phil 3:17-19); "so put to death the things in you which are earthly: sexual immorality, uncleanness, passion, evil desire, and greed (which is idolatry)—on account of these the wrath of God is coming" (Col 3:5-6); "let no one cross any boundary or take advantage of a brother or sister in the matter, seeing as the Lord is an avenger in all these things, just as we have warned you before" (1 Thess 4:6); "but if someone does not want to obey our instruction in this letter . . . do not think of them as enemies but warn them as fellow disciples" (2 Thess 4:14-15); "I command you . . . to obey the commandment, spotless and above reproach, until the appearance of our Lord Jesus Christ" (1 Tim 6:13-14); "Alexander the coppersmith did many evil things to me, the Lord will pay him back for what he has done" (2 Tim 4:14); "for the grace of God has appeared . . . teaching us . . . that we should live practicing self-control, righteously, and in a godly way . . . as we wait for the blessed hope and appearance of the glory of our great God and savior Jesus Christ" (Titus 2:11-13).[21] Paul encourages the early Christian communities to live holy lives in the light of Christ coming again to judge.

But for Paul this is not bad news or onerous on Christian believers because our becoming holy is the work *of Christ* (1 Cor 1:4-9):

> I am always giving thanks to God about you for the grace of God given to you in Christ Jesus, 5 because you have been enriched in him in all speech and in all knowledge, 6 just as the testimony

---

21. The only letter in which I cannot find an obvious reference to behaving in the light of the coming of Christ is Philemon. Otherwise, the motif appears in every other Pauline letter at least once. I acknowledge that not all New Testament scholars accept that all the epistles I quote here are written by Paul. However, the point I am making remains unaffected. However many Pauline letters are chopped off the list, the fact is that all the ones that remain on the list (except Philemon) speak of leading holy lives in the light of the coming of Christ to judge—unless anyone suggests that the only indubitable Pauline is Philemon, and I am unaware of anyone who argues this case. For those who may wish to review the arguments for paulinicity of disputed letters: on Ephesians, for an argument that it is Pauline, see O'Brien, *Ephesians*, 4-47; for an argument against, see Best, *Ephesians*, 6-36; on Colossians, for an argument that it is Pauline, see Moo, *Colossians*, 28-41; for an argument against, see McL. Wilson, *Colossians and Philemon*, 8-35; on 2 Thessalonians, for an argument that it is Pauline, see Malherbe, *Thessalonians*, 349-75; for an argument against, see Richard, *Thessalonians*, 19-29; on 1 and 2 Timothy, for an argument that they are Pauline, see Johnson, *Letters to Timothy*, 55-90; for an argument against, see Marshall, *Pastoral Epistles*, 57-92; on Titus, for an argument that it is Pauline, see Towner, *Timothy and Titus*, 9-89; for an argument against, see Dibelius and Conzelmann, *Pastoral Epistles*, 1-10.

> about Christ has been made firm in you, 7 so that you are not lacking in any spiritual gift as you eagerly await the revelation of our Lord Jesus Christ, 8 who will also make you firm until the end, blameless on the day of our Lord Jesus Christ. 9 God is faithful—through him you have been called into fellowship with his Son Jesus Christ our Lord.

The Christians at the church in Corinth have not enriched themselves in speech and knowledge. They have not strengthened themselves in the testimony about Christ. *God* has done all this in them. As they await the day when Christ comes again to judge the world, it is *Jesus* who prepares them for that day. Literally, "he will confirm you blameless" (1 Cor 1:8). Paul has a clear hope that Jesus himself will make the Corinthian Christians blameless on the day of the Lord. This is quite a statement, given the moral challenges which Paul presents to the Corinthian church later in the letter (e.g., to stop breaking into factions, to stop engaging in various kinds of sexually immoral behavior, to stop taking part in idolatrous practices, and to stop using their spiritual gifts to gain some sense of superiority over others).[22] Despite all this, Paul states that he expects that Jesus will make them morally blameless for that day, and Paul believes that this is the work of Christ in them.[23]

Similarly, in Ephesians, Paul makes a statement that demonstrates his assumption that Jesus himself teaches Christian believers how to live holy lives (Eph 4:17–21a):[24]

> Therefore I say this and I testify in the Lord, that you should no longer walk as the gentiles walk in the emptiness of their thinking, 18 being darkened in their minds, alienated from life of

---

22. Fitzmyer, *First Corinthians*, 133.

23. Fee, *First Corinthians*, 43–44. Fee argues for God making the Corinthian Christians firm and blameless (along with other modern commentators) despite the fact that the immediate antecedent of the verb is Jesus Christ. Given that the immediate antecedent of the verb is Jesus Christ and the text reads "of Jesus Christ who also makes firm . . . ," it seems most natural to read Paul as stating that Jesus makes them blameless. Thiselton (*First Corinthians*, 101) comments, "after reviewing the exhaustive discussions . . . [the issue] . . . 'cannot be decided unequivocally.'" On another point, Paul can hardly mean that Christ will make them blameless only by his death on the cross and without addressing their behavior. If he did mean this, he would not have needed to write to them about addressing their sinful behavior and could simply have assured them of their salvation despite their continuing in sin.

24. Again, I assume Ephesians is Pauline. For another defense of this view, see Hoehner, *Ephesians*, 2–61.

> God because of the ignorance that is in them and because of the hardness of their hearts, 19 who having lost all sensitivity handed themselves over to debauchery, greedy to indulge in every impurity. 20 But that is not the way that you learned Christ, 21 if you really heard him and were taught by him . . . .[25]

Within the New Testament, this is the only place where anyone talks of learning Christ. The phrase sounds odd because people do not ordinarily learn other people but learn about them. Paul does not speak of knowledge about Christ here but of getting to know Jesus Christ personally.[26] Within this personal relationship, disciples hear Jesus as they are taught by him.[27] What Jesus promised his disciples (Matt 11:29), Paul understands to be their reality—that Jesus teaches them each individually in gentleness and humility how to live out his commands.

So, Paul does not set up an alternative gospel to the one Jesus preaches. Paul believes that people find forgiveness of sins through all Christ achieved by his death on the cross. He also calls Christian believers to lives of holiness. Not only does he spell out in many practical situations what this means for particular Christian communities and individuals in his letters, but more generally he writes that those baptized into Christ are committed to living out the form of teaching to which they have been entrusted (Rom 6:17)—in other words, to living out the teachings of Jesus.[28] He repeatedly encourages Christians away from sinful living because of the fact that one day Christ will come again to judge. He wants people to obey Christ. He does not preach a commandment-free pseudo-gospel of "love" received.[29] Instead, he teaches that Christ himself enables Christian believers to live out the lives to which he calls them.

So, Jesus turns out to be someone whom I suspect many Christians today and down the centuries knew all along. He is committed to his disciples and promises to be present with them all day every day as they follow

---

25. I translate the *en autō*, v. 21, as an instrumental dative "by him." For brief comments on the difficulties of the dative *en*, see Best, *Ephesians*, 428.

26. Best, *Ephesians*, 426–27; Hoehner, *Ephesians*, 594.

27. The Greek clearly means "heard him" (so Best, *Ephesians*, 427). Translating "heard about him" (e.g., NRSV; Hoehner, *Ephesians*, 594) is not only inaccurate but unnecessary. The believer hears the voice of the one true teacher teaching them God's ways.

28. For the various options for interpreting Rom 6:17, including this one, see Fitzmyer, *Romans*, 449–50; and Longenecker, *Romans*, 622–27.

29. Which is rather closer to divine moral collusion with sinful humanity than forgiveness and reconciliation in Christ.

his command to make disciples of all peoples. In his earthly ministry, he gave the ultimate interpretation of the Torah and has identified this as the law. But he did not and does not leave his disciples to learn how to live out his teaching by themselves—let alone to teach it to others in their own strength or weakness. He commits himself to teach personally each disciple how to live out his commands, and he promises to do this in humility and gentleness as he comes alongside us. He will never leave us as we learn from him how to live his way. He also commits to being the real teacher as we engage in teaching others to obey his commands. He knows our frailty and arrogance. So, he teaches us to sort our own lives out before we try sorting out problems in others with which we struggle ourselves. We need not fret or fear that he has come to fulfill the law because he has not come to tell us to fulfill it by our own efforts. He has committed to fulfilling this law in us through his gentle and humble mentoring of us. And he calls us to become a community of humble fellow disciples who acknowledge our own strengths and weaknesses, and who seek to encourage one another in kindness and integrity.

5

Five (Dirty) Words Every Christian Needs to Learn

Jesus longs to come alongside us to help us to learn how to live out his life-giving teaching. He calls us to repentance, to seek his forgiveness of our sins and his help to turn our lives around. His understanding of repentance involves a change in the way we *think* and a change in the way we *act*. We need to want to love God above all things and to love our neighbors as ourselves. If we love God we will obey Jesus' commands, as they simply spell out what it means to love God with all our heart, mind, soul, and strength, and to love our neighbors as ourselves. Jesus promises to be with us every minute of every day as we learn from him how to do all this in practice. He also promises to be with us as the one true teacher as we join in his ministry of teaching all the nations to obey everything he has commanded. We will not remain the same as we learn from him. His teaching us and our learning from him are transformative. We do not simply learn about the things Jesus taught or about his vision of the kingdom of God. We live out his teachings and we become the people through whom he gives others the hope of entering the kingdom of God. Jesus seeks obedient disciples, not people who think they know him—however impressed they are by the ministries they perform in his name. Becoming an obedient disciple cannot be anything other than transforming because we change in the process of learning. We change the way we think. We change our values. We change the way we act. And all this happens through our closely following and humbly learning from the living Lord who loves us and never leaves us this side of judgment day.

Five (dirty) words every Christian needs to learn

None of this happens without a change of mind and heart on our part. Basic to this change of heart is that we accept the commands of Jesus and the life to which he calls us. Some of this is quite counter-cultural. However, just because something Jesus teaches us does not sit easily with us (at least, initially) or with our culture does not mean it is not true. In his final words in the Gospel story (Matt 28:16–20), we find five things in Jesus' commands that many contemporary people (including people of faith) might find uncomfortable and difficult to accept.

> And the eleven disciples went to Galilee to the mountain that Jesus had commanded them to go to, 17 and seeing him they worshipped him, although some doubted. 18 And coming towards them Jesus spoke to them, "All authority in heaven and on earth has been given to me. 19 Therefore go, make disciples of all the nations: baptizing them into the name of the Father, and the Son, and the Holy Spirit; 20 teaching them to obey all the things I have commanded you, and look, I will be with you every day until the end of the age.

These five things might be listed in five words: authority, teach, obey, command, and judgment. Within contemporary Western culture these have become dirty words because they threaten our autonomy, the right that our culture teaches us we have to decide for ourselves exactly what we will think, say, and do. Anything that looks like it might stop us exercising this right tends to raise our eyebrows, if not our hackles. Jesus' words here cut straight across many of the ideas of autonomy that we imbibe from the culture around us. However, Jesus speaks these words to all his disciples—making these five (possibly dirty) words every Christian needs to learn.

Authority

Jesus claims that all authority in heaven and on earth has been given to him. This claim would be outrageous were it not true. Only God rules over heaven and earth. So, by stating that he has been given all this authority, Jesus implies that he is God, or at the very least, in some way or other, a divine being alongside God with God-given authority to rule over everything on behalf of God. His words are very reminiscent of a scene in the court room of heaven found in the book of Daniel (Dan 7:13–14), where the divine figure of the Son of Man enters heaven on clouds and is given all authority by the Ancient of Days seated on the throne of heaven.[1] Jesus has referred to himself as the Son of Man throughout the Gospel.[2] He has stated that God is the Father of the Son of Man (Matt 16:27), so the Son of Man must be the Son of God the Father.[3] Therefore, in Matthew 28, the Father appears to take the role that the Ancient of Days takes in Daniel 7. He gives all authority in heaven and on earth to Jesus because Jesus is the Son of Man.

In the vision in Daniel 7, the "one like a son of man" receives authority so that all the peoples, tribes, and tongues serve him, or worship him (the verb carries both meanings in Aramaic, the language in which Daniel 7 was written). The image is of universal dominion in which the one like a son of man becomes the ruler of the whole world. Accordingly, everyone in the world serves him. So, the echoes of Daniel 7 in Jesus' words "all authority in heaven and on earth has been given to me" imply that Jesus has authority over every culture and subculture in every human society. In other words, Jesus has the right to lay down the law. He makes the rules. From the perspective of any of us who want to live according to our own rules,

---

1. This is made clear by the fact that Matt 28:18–20 bears three verbal similarities to Daniel 7:13–14 LXX: "is given" (Greek *edothē*), "authority" (*exousia*), and "all the nations/gentiles" (*panta ta ethnē*), as well as the same word order (*edothē* + dative pronoun + *exousia*), making it reasonable to assume that Matt 28:18–20 recalls Dan 7:13–14 (so Davies and Allison, *Matthew*, 3:682–83). For those who know the Septuagint and its variants, I freely admit that the Greek translation of Dan 7:13–14 by Theodotion comes much closer to the original Aramaic, which reads: "I was watching in visions of the night and look, one like a son of man was coming with the clouds of heaven and he came up to the ancient of days and was presented before him, 14 and then he was given dominion and honor and kingdom, and all the peoples, tribes, and tongues served (or worshipped) him, his dominion is an everlasting dominion that will not pass away and his kingdom is one that shall not be destroyed," and so is not quite so close to the text of Matthew.

2. For the Son of Man sayings in Matthew, see Matt 8:20; 9:26; 10:23; 11:19; 12:8, 32, 40; 13:37, 41; 16:13, 27–28; 17:9, 12, 22; 19:28; 20:18, 28; 24:27, 30, 37, 39, 44; 25:31; 26:2, 24, 45, 64.

3. In Matt 16:27, Jesus says that "the Son of Man is going to come in the glory of his Father," which implies that the Father is the father of the Son of Man. As the Father can be none other than God, then the Son of Man must be the Son of God in the understanding of the Matthean Jesus.

this can feel threatening. Politically, it can appear deeply subversive. It does not simply suggest but states outright that Jesus has the right to overrule the laws made by parliaments and governments around the world. Where their laws clash with the teachings of Jesus, Jesus is right and they are wrong. Where Jesus' teachings clash with cultural trends, his teachings are true and the cultural trends are mistaken. In societies, like many Western societies today, this feels wrong to many Christian disciples, as we are accustomed to our religious faith belonging only to the "spiritual" sphere. Even where we say it applies to everyday life, most of us would not dream of contravening a rule or practice at work because Jesus taught differently. We are used to finding reasons for why we ought not to put Jesus' teachings into practice. For example, one idea that has filtered down from the world of academic theology to popular Christianity is: "that command no longer applies because it is cultural." If something in Jesus' teaching is deemed to belong to the ancient culture of Jesus' day, we say it no longer applies because things that were cultural then do not apply now.[4] However, our application of this principle is not even-handed. No one ever applies this to the commands "You shall love the Lord your God with all your heart and with all your soul and with all your mind" or "You shall love your neighbor as yourself," suggesting that they no longer apply, despite the fact that these two commands were deeply cultural at the time of Jesus, having been embedded in the ancient culture of Jews for hundreds of years before Jesus was born. We can tend to seek and find interpretations of Jesus' words that enable us to do what we feel or think is right instead.[5]

At the heart of the issue seems to lie a reluctance to accept authority. There are areas in life where many of us accept that someone has authority over a limited part of our lives and for a limited time. For example, when we enter employment we accept (at least to some degree) that the boss is the boss and we must do as they may reasonably require at work. If we take classes in anything, from Spanish to swimming, we know that we have

---

4. Just to clarify, I do not wish to dismiss for one minute the importance of hermeneutics. I simply want to point out the ease with which many people dismiss the teachings of Jesus and the rest of the New Testament without very much intelligent thought, and to state that this is not very conducive to healthy discipleship. For any who want to follow this up, a classic statement of the issues of how Christians relate the gospel within and to their own "contemporary" cultures may be found in Niebuhr, *Christ and Culture*. I read Jesus as stating that his teachings stand for all time, and a key message of this book is that we need to listen again to Jesus' presentation of the enduring authority of his teaching.

5. You could be forgiven for suggesting that we run the risk of developing hermeneutics of anti-discipleship.

something to learn from the teacher or trainer and so accept their authority in their helping us to get better at that activity. However, it is deeply counter-cultural to accept that anyone has authority over us everywhere and all the time, let alone in all areas of our lives. In our heart of hearts, many of us feel that not even Almighty God has that right—and this is precisely the issue. Almighty God does have that right, and as God the Father he has granted that right to his Son Jesus Christ, the Son of Man: "All authority on heaven and on earth has been given to me" (Matt 28:18). Without accepting that the Lord Jesus Christ has that right and authority, there can be little progress in Christian discipleship.[6] Without accepting his authority, calling him "Lord, Lord" is meaningless, as the very word "Lord" implies that we recognize his authority and that we have committed to serve him. Yet we have less to fear than we might sometimes think in accepting the authority of Jesus. His promise to all disciples is to exercise this authority in coming alongside us in humility and gentleness. He exercises his authority *in self-giving love.*

Teach

In the world of contemporary education, there seem to be many more popular words than "teach." People today prefer to be "educated" or, better still, "enabled." We like to "explore" and "discover" things for ourselves. We can even tire of or become disgruntled by people who try to "facilitate" us.

---

6. There have been attempts to revise this traditional understanding of Jesus' authority. In his classic popularization of twentieth-century liberal theology, *Honest to God*, John A. T. Robinson argued that the authority of God and the right of every human being to decide for themselves were one and the same (especially, pp. 105–21). Writing for a society that had opted for the right of everyone to make their own moral choices rather than follow the teachings of Jesus, he suggested that God's commands and human moral choice met at the point where people discovered their true humanity. In his words, heteronomy and autonomy met in theonomy (*Honest to God*, 113–15). He berated traditionalist Christians for clinging to an idea of God up in heaven giving us moral commands, stating that we could not blame society for moving on from this kind of naïve religious faith after the moral revolution of the 1960s. If Christian faith were to grow, the new generation needed new theological expression of that faith. Since he wrote, there has not been a notable explosion of new liberal churches winning *any* Western nation to this particular revision of traditional Christianity. Alasdair MacIntyre was the prophet here ("God and the Theologians," 215–28) when he stated that there was so little difference between Robinson's picture of Christianity and existentialism that nobody would be won to faith by the theology of *Honest to God*. MacIntyre himself later converted to Roman Catholicism.

Five (Dirty) Words Every Christian Needs to Learn

We suspect that, underneath it all, they really have an agenda and we tend to find that our expectations are rarely disappointed. It seems that we like to be the judge of whether something is true or not. Increasingly, it does not matter whether we have the relevant qualifications to judge whether something is true or false either. Our respect for authority has diminished sufficiently that we readily dismiss any expert should their teaching, or facilitation, or advice not meet with our approval. If anyone is to get anything across to us, they need to win us over first. We far more readily believe an attractive character than we do someone who might know what they are talking about.

So, "teach" is not necessarily a popular word today. Teaching suggests an authority figure who has a set of ideas and an endgame that we should come to believe their set of ideas. They believe that their ideas are true and that we need to know the truth. They may approach teaching us this truth in a variety of ways, using various teaching methods, but ultimately the goal remains the same: that we believe their truth. As students we have even learned to distinguish between the teacher with the attractive character and the truths they are trying to teach us. We may like them as people, we may even admire them, but we retain the right to be highly suspicious of anything they try to get us to believe—unless it is something we want to hear or already believe.

Jesus Christ claims to be *the* authoritative teacher. Christian discipleship cannot even start unless we are willing to learn from him (and this includes new ways of behaving) because discipleship is precisely about learning from the one true teacher. However, he promises to enable us and to come alongside us all day every day in order to help us learn. He commits to teaching us in humility of mind and heart, and with gentleness and compassion. He also has an advantage over many other moral teachers in that he is without sin. Nobody can reasonably charge him with hypocrisy. He has lived the life he invites us to learn to live. In that sense, he is an attractive character as he leads from the front and has the humility to come down to our level without making a big thing of it. Even so, he does not invite us to write the moral curriculum with him. He does teach truth, and he not only wants us to *believe* the truth but to learn to *live it out in practice*. In doing this, he wants us to un-learn and disown other ideas we may previously have held to be true, and to un-learn certain ways of behaving that are not right and good. In all of this, he promises to be present with us, constantly helping us every step along the way.

The Jesus You *Really* Didn't Know

Obey

Obedience is not only an unpopular word today but a word people dislike, or even despise. Obedience cannot help but carry the implication that someone else has the right to tell us what to do. Anyone who has taken marriage preparation classes in any Christian church where there is the option for the wife-to-be to promise to obey will know just how much horror the very idea of committing ourselves to being obedient to somebody else can cause. We might love somebody so much that we will commit to spend the rest of our lives with them, we will promise to be with them for worse, for poorer, and in sickness, we might even be willing to go to the ends of the earth for them, but there is no way in God's heaven we would ever consider being obedient to them. The idea of obedience rankles more than most. Obedience has also been abused where people have taken the obedience of others as an excuse and opportunity to bully them. Understandably, those who have suffered such abuse can be wary of obedience.

One of the reasons that obedience seems to offend people so much today is that it cuts right across our autonomy, our right to choose who we are, and how we think, speak, and act. Teaching may be an offense to our autonomy, but at least it has the virtue of being an attack from the outside. Someone else is trying to tell us what to do or what to think. I suspect the reason that some people find obedience so unpalatable is that they feel or believe that obedience is a betrayal of themselves. If they obey, they have given up their right to choose who they are, and how they think, speak, and act. Given that so many people today almost idolize their "right" to be themselves, obeying somebody else seems like giving up their identity. If we obey, we cease to be human because we no longer decide for ourselves.

Admittedly, the Greek word Jesus uses in the offending statement is actually "keep" (*tērein*) rather than the normal word for "obey" (*hypakouein*). However, only a theological weasel would try to wriggle out of the offense caused by the idea of obedience by playing that kind of word game here. Jesus tells his disciples to make disciples "teaching them to *keep* all the things which I have commanded you" (Matt 28:20). The meaning of *terein* here is clearly "obey," as keeping a command involves obedience to the command. Jesus does require obedience: "everyone who hears my words and puts them into practice may be likened to a wise man . . . and everyone who hears my words and does not put them into practice may be likened to a foolish man . . ." (Matt 7:24, 26). The person who hears his words and does them is his disciple (Matt 12:50) whereas he will say that he never knew those who do not follow his commands (Matt 7:23). There really can be no genuine Christian discipleship without obedience. However, this obedience is to a God who is always good, and not obedience to a tyrant or a bully. Jesus demonstrates his compassion in living with us, in all of our struggles, and gently enabling us day by day to live out the lives of love to which he calls us. Jesus is present with us in all he calls us to be and do, and he loves us.

Command

Contemporary society prefers the word "option" to the word "command." Most people like to be offered a series of choices from which they may select their preference. People value their freedom and so want to be able to choose. The idea that our freedom to choose for ourselves should be withdrawn goes against the grain. The very notion of command does precisely that. Commands instruct people what they should do. The idea of "command" cuts across our right to choose for ourselves how we think, speak, and act. A dominant myth in society today is that the most loving thing that any one human being can do for another is to give them their freedom to choose how they live. Consequently, for many today, the issuing of commands feels not only like inappropriate behavior but a profoundly unloving way of acting.

However, Jesus does command that we act in certain ways and he expects us to live out his teaching. He tells his disciples that those who break even the least of God's commandments will be called least in the kingdom of heaven (Matt 5:19). He instructs people he meets in the course of his ministry to obey God's commands (e.g., Matt 8:4). He upbraids people for failing to obey God's commandments as they pursue their own moral ideas and agendas (Matt 15:3). Indeed, Jesus told his disciples to teach all the nations to obey his commands (Matt 28:20). Attempting to be a disciple of Jesus without taking his commands seriously makes no sense. Jesus himself says that to any who try this, he will respond on judgment day: "I never knew you; depart from me, you workers of lawlessness" (Matt 7:23).

However, none of this suggests that Jesus is unloving. Nothing could be further from the truth. Jesus teaches that all his commands hang on love of God and neighbor (Matt 22:37–40).[7] Jesus understands that love is cen-

---

7. Technically, Jesus taught that all the law and the prophets hung on these two commands. As Jesus equates his teaching with the law (e.g., "my yoke" in Matt 11:29) and

tral to the law and every prophetic call to bring people back to obedience to the law. Or, as the situation is now for Christians, love is central to Jesus' teaching and any prophetic call to Christians to come back into obedience to his teaching. Ironically, as Jesus makes these two commands central to his understanding of obedience, any loveless and lifeless drudging "obedience" to his commands cannot be obedience to Jesus as there is no love in the obedience. True obedience comes from a heart and mind filled with love for God and neighbor, from which arises the desire to love God and neighbor in practice. As Jesus put it elsewhere, "if you love me, you will keep my commandments" (John 14:15). Obedience flows naturally from genuine commitment to Jesus in the life of discipleship. After all, there is no such thing as love for Jesus that does not result in obedience to his commands. That kind of love is love of self and love of what we can get out of Jesus—and that is something quite different.

Judgment

"Judge ye not lest ye be judged" are some of the most misquoted words from the whole Bible. These words are often uttered as an attempt at rebuke by people who do not like the moral ideas, judgments, or opinions of others. The purpose of (mis)quoting Jesus' words is to lend authority to their desire that the person whose ideas offend them should remain silent on whatever they are talking about, and preferably withdraw their statements with an apology. It is deeply ironic that anybody should ever have chosen to misquote Jesus in order to try to make this kind of point because judgment was absolutely central to Jesus' understanding of everything.[8]

---

that he fulfills the law and the prophets in his teaching ministry (Matt 5:17), I am happy to summarize the situation as I have done above.

8. For understanding why this is a misquotation, see the discussion of Matt 7:1–5 on pp. 67–69 above. Briefly, this negative command introduces his teaching about taking logs out of one's own eye *before* trying to take the speck out of somebody else's eye. This teaching is not designed to prevent people from helping others to grow morally but to ensure that they have already developed the moral character necessary for the task. Note that Jesus gives an explanation for why one should not judge in case one is judged: "*for by the judgment with which you judge others, you will be judged; and by the measure with which you measure others, you will be measured*" (Matt 7:2). The command is not absolute but advisory: not "absolutely never do this" but "watch it, because if you do this, that will happen to you." Hence, this teaching is followed by "so get your act together before you try to help anyone else."

Jesus' whole ministry revolves around the idea of judgment. His call to repentance (e.g., Matt 4:17) presumes that there will be divine judgment, and repentance is necessary so that people might stand forgiven before the judgment seat of God. Jesus teaches people so that they may know and practice God's commands, and not be turned away from the kingdom of heaven on that day as "workers of lawlessness" (Matt 7:23). The reality of the judgment of God on all humanity lies right at the heart of Jesus' understanding and practice of ministry. Jesus' final words in the Gospel of Matthew (which are the final words of this gospel) remind his disciples of the fact that God will come to judge. He promises to be with his disciples "until the end of the age" (Matt 28:20). The phrase "the end of the age" (Greek *synteleia tou aiōnos*) reminds the reader of the day of judgment, because Jesus only ever uses these words to refer to that particular event (Matt 13:40, 49). So, with his final words, Jesus reminds his disciples that the day of judgment ought to remain a key focus for their thinking and ministry. No Christian disciple can avoid or sideline judgment on account of any contemporary moral distaste for the idea. If it was central to Jesus' thinking, it ought to be the same for his disciples.

But this ought not to worry people. People long for justice. The fact that contemporary Western society has become increasingly litigious over the past four or five decades bears witness to this fact. People take each other to court, people take institutions like health services and companies to court, people take the police to court and not infrequently consider legal challenges against the government—all because we desire justice. The judgment of God will be the ultimate act of justice. Every wrong ever committed will be righted once and for all. Every corrupt government will face the due penalty. Every unjust institution will be held to account. Everyone who has wronged us will face justice. This should be a reason for great celebration, as truth will come out and all will be judged, punished, and vindicated according to what is true. When the truth of the judgment is grasped, no one can reasonably argue that God is anything but loving as he demonstrates his love in giving us the justice we all desire.

On the other hand, precisely this is very worrying for all who have committed any wrong against another person—regardless of whether they committed the wrong through personal desire, or as a result of carrying out the unjust activities of a company, institution, or government. Justice is all very well and good when the judge metes justice upon someone else. It is rather less comfortable when *we* are the recipients of the penalties for our own sins. But even this ought not to be a cause for worry. The point of Jesus' death to forgive us is to take the punishment for our sins so that we might live free from fear of punishment. His promise to be with us all day every day until the end of the age is precisely to prepare us for that final judgment and lead us out of unholy lives into living in ways that bless others and honor God. That is why Jesus offers to teach us how to obey his commands.

Paul understood what was necessary for Christian disciples to grow, as he instructed them not to allow themselves to be shaped by the cultures of this world but to be radically changed by the renewal of their minds so that they might know God's will—his good, pleasing, and perfect will (Rom 12:2). Basic to lives of true worship, and fundamental to Christian discipleship, is allowing God to renew our minds. This means discerning the will of God and that will entail rejecting at least some of what our cultures teach us. Jesus puts things more simply, and specifically. Rather than leaving the theological wiggle room that inevitably flows from using phrases like Paul's "discerning the will of God," Jesus simply tells people to obey his commands. Accepting his authority, and his teaching, and living in obedience to his commands requires a change of mind, heart, and practice for many of us who claim to be Christian disciples. Holding God's judgment of all humanity as central to our way of looking at the world and organizing how we live, again requires something of a refocusing of our values and priorities. Unless we do these things, we cannot live as disciples of Christ. Until we do them, we cannot engage in the ministry and mission to which he calls us. Within the culture of "lifestyle Christianity" the terms "authority," "teach," "obey," "command," and "judgment" have become not only rare but dirty words. Every Christian disciple who wants to take Jesus' understanding of discipleship, mission, and ministry at all seriously, needs to learn (or re-learn) them. But re-learning them is not something we do on our own, nor is it an impossible task. God himself in Jesus Christ comes alongside us in all our struggles and teaches us day by day, in all our stumbling, how to live the life to which he calls us all—and he brings us into the community of his disciples so we can learn alongside others who share the same path, same struggles, and same goals.

A learning community of humility and forgiveness

Jesus calls us to learn (or re-learn) this language of faith, both in community and in practice. Matthew chapter 18 offers a succinct account of his teaching on living together and learning together in community. It has been suggested that this chapter concerns church discipline, but Jesus' teaching here goes wider than that.[9] It explores and explains how a community of disciples are to take practical steps to grow together in grace, humility, holiness, and forgiveness. Handling disagreements, relationship breakdown, and living in such a way that we do not cause other people moral difficulties are some of the topics covered. Jesus' teaching on these topics can come across as so straight-talking as to feel severe. However, at the center of all of these topics, lies the gentleness, grace, and forgiveness in which Jesus calls us to live together.

Humility

> At that time the disciples came to Jesus and said, "But who is the greatest in the kingdom of heaven?" 2 And calling over a child he stood him [or her] in the middle of them 3 and said, "I tell you straight, unless you turn around and become like children, you will not enter the kingdom of heaven. 4 So, whoever humbles themselves like this child, they are the greatest in the kingdom of heaven. 5 And whoever accepts one child like this in my name, accepts me. (Matt 18:1–5)

The disciples ask Jesus the question: "who is greatest in the kingdom of heaven?" (The phrases "the kingdom of God" and "the kingdom of heaven" sometimes functioned as shorthand for the restored kingdom of Israel, free from political domination by any other nation.) Various passages in the New Testament give us the impression that the disciples were expecting a revolution in Israel that would put Jesus on the throne of David and put them in positions of political power.[10] Some of them were not above sidling up to Jesus to ask for the most powerful positions in government (Mark 10:35–37 and Matt 20:20–23, where James' and John's mother asks for them). So, there is every reason to suppose this question concerns who amongst the disciples will hold the most powerful offices of state in the new kingdom of Israel.[11] Jesus responds with something of an acted parable.

---

9. Hagner, *Matthew 14–18*, 514; Turner, *Matthew*, 431.

10. For example, Acts 1:6, where the disciples ask Jesus "Lord, is it in this time that you are going to restore the kingdom to Israel?" They clearly expect Jesus to fulfill their visions of an Israel without Rome (so, e.g., Fitzmyer, *Acts*, 205).

11. Given the similarity with the question of James' and John's mother (Matt 20:20–23), which clearly concerns the restored kingdom of Israel (so, e.g., Davies and Allison,

He calls over a child. We do not know whether it was a girl or a boy, but he stands this child in the middle of the disciples and tells them that unless they become like children they will never even *enter* the kingdom of heaven (let alone hold any position of political power within it).[12] Children held no political power.

Jesus requires a change in his disciples. They are to turn around, to change their attitudes and outlook. He knows that they want to be great (if not the greatest) in the new and coming kingdom of Israel. So, he teaches them two things. First that they are to become humble like the child he has placed in the middle of them. The child would have had no political power or even authority within their own family. That does not mean that this child had a rotten life. They may well have been much loved and greatly cared for by their parents. The point is, they had no power. They were genuinely humble. Jesus calls his disciples to choose to become humble like this child rather than to seek power within the community he was forming. He does not call those who hold leadership within his community to seek power. Rather, they should seek humility.

The second change Jesus requires in his disciples concerns the way they view others. He tells his disciples that if they receive a "child like this" in his name, they receive him. The "child like this" refers to Jesus' disciples, to those who are humbling themselves like children.[13] None of the disciples would question the importance of accepting Jesus. Therefore, by identifying

---

Matthew, 3:88), I can see no reason to read this question differently—despite the fact that many commentators wonder whether the kingdom of heaven here refers to the end of time or the church (so, e.g., Davies and Allison, *Matthew*, 2:756; Gundry, *Matthew*, 359; Luz, *Matthew 8–20*, 426). The fact that Jesus turns the topic of conversation into relationships of humility and forgiveness in the community he calls around him does not change the fact that the starting point of this conversation was the disciples' desire for power in the new Israel.

12. The words in brackets are implicit in what Jesus said.

13. There is a debate about whether the "child like this" in v. 5 refers to an actual child like the one standing in the middle of the disciples or a disciple of Christ. Some argue that the child must refer back to the child in v. 3 and that Jesus means "like this" in the sense "the one standing in the middle of us" (so, e.g., Davies and Allison, *Matthew*, 3:759). Others argue that "like this" refers back to v. 4 and has the sense "children like the ones who are humbling themselves like children" and so refers to disciples of Christ (Hagner, *Matthew 14–28*, 521). Some hedge their bets and opt for both interpretations (e.g., France, *Matthew*, 679). I find the argument that v. 5 refers back to v. 4 more persuasive because not only does it make sense but it leads more naturally into v. 6 than the alternative reading. The fact that it fits the whole context better makes it the reading to be preferred.

himself with his disciples, Jesus teaches how important it is for the disciples to accept each other. Rather than jostling or vying for power amongst themselves (or worse, doing it behind each other's backs and through third parties), the disciples ought to become humble and accept one another. When they do that, they will find that they are accepting Jesus.

Jesus does not ask anything of his disciples here which he has not shown himself willing to do. He has already taught them to learn from him because he is meek and humble in heart and mind (Matt 11:29). Despite the fact that Jesus is the divine Son of Man who has received all power and authority over all the nations from God the Father, he humbles himself by coming alongside the individual disciple to help them to learn how to live out his teaching. He promises to be present with each of his disciples all day every day, teaching how to live (Matt 28:20). He comes alongside us and gives us quite literally all the time in the world.

Within this short conversation we move from the power fantasies of the disciples to the nature of the community Jesus leads. Contemporary Christians are no less prone to power fantasies (political and otherwise) than were those first disciples. The language of changing politics and transforming society can be found across the whole spectrum of church traditions today, and much of it concerns changing society to fit our various political visions without necessarily consulting anyone else (other than those in our own religious and political group) as to whether they want us to drive our policies into laws they must observe. Within some churches, we seem to have learned some of the worst aspects of political correctness. Jesus cuts these power fantasies down to size by teaching us to become like those who have no vote (i.e., children).[14] We need to do this to even enter the kingdom of heaven. Humility is an entrance requirement, at least, so thinks Jesus. When we truly humble ourselves in this way, then we show true greatness. As we learn this kind of humility, we drop our desires to exercise control over others within the Christian community. We accept others as fellow disciples of Christ and make no attempt to exercise power over them. In fact, we make ourselves powerless, open, and vulnerable amongst them. This is what accepting Jesus means.

---

14. Not that anyone in Judea had the vote in the first century AD.

The Jesus You *Really* Didn't Know

Taking care

> Whoever makes one of these little ones who believe in me fall into sin, it would be better for them that they hung a large millstone around their necks and they drowned in the depths of the sea. 7 Causes of falling into sin bring woe to the world, for causes for falling into sin are bound to occur. However, woe to the person through whom the causes for falling into sin come about. 8 But if your hand or your foot causes you to fall into sin, cut it off and throw it away from yourself. It is better to enter life crippled or lame than to be thrown in the eternal fire with two hands or two feet. 9 And if your eye causes you to fall into sin, cut it out and throw it away from yourself. It is better to enter life one-eyed than to be thrown into the hell of fire with two eyes. (Matt 18:6–9)

The warnings in this text are dire. The person who causes anyone else to fall into sin would do well to hang a millstone around their necks and drown themselves in the depths of the sea, as this end would be preferable to the judgment they will incur for making any who follow Jesus fall into sin. Anyone causing one of his disciples to fall into sin is in deep trouble. It does not matter that there are plenty of temptations in the world already, they are still in deep trouble for causing a follower of Jesus Christ to sin. If physical temptations of any nature are too much for us to bear and the relevant part of our body is just itching to fall into sin (hand, foot, or eye here), then we do better to cut it off or out in order to avoid succumbing to the temptation and reaping the reward of eternal punishment in hell.[15]

The warnings may be softened to some extent by arguing that Jesus was exaggerating to drive the point home. He tells people to cut off their hands and feet or cut out their eyes, if they caused them to sin, and enter eternal life crippled, lame, or one-eyed rather than go be thrown into the hell of fire. There is a good reason for making the assumption that Jesus exaggerated to make his point here. He shared the hope of the resurrection from the dead with some other Jews of his day (e.g., Matt 22:23–32). The belief was that on the day of resurrection those who were righteous would enter eternal life and that their resurrection bodies would be whole (e.g., 2 Macc 7:1–40).[16] Therefore, it is very unlikely that Jesus envisaged the

---

15. Davies and Allison, *Matthew*, 2.761–75.

16. These verses describe the martyrdom of seven Jewish brothers at the hands of the Greek tyrant Antiochus IV Epiphanes. The second and fourth brothers affirm their hope of resurrection (2 Macc 7:9, 14). Their mother affirms her hope for their resurrection which she clearly assumes will be physical (2 Macc 7:23, 29). The third brother affirms

Five (Dirty) Words Every Christian Needs to Learn

righteous living eternally with dismemberment. Consequently, he probably did not seriously expect anyone to enter life crippled, lame, or one-eyed, which blunts the force his exhortations to cut out eyes or cut off limbs, if he meant them to be taken literally. Rather, he uses the graphic image to shock his hearers into taking holiness seriously.

Jesus calls his disciples to holiness in two ways here. He calls them to personal holiness and to make the radical changes in their lives that mean that they will not fall prey to temptation and stray into sinful ways of behaving. He also calls them to behave in ways that ensure that they in no way cause or encourage their Christian brothers and sisters to sin. Despite the fierce nature of the language and the graphic imagery of bodily self-mutilation, there is love and goodness at the heart of these sayings. Jesus wants his disciples to live out his commands in lives of love towards themselves and towards each other. He wants his disciples to take others so seriously that they do all they can to help them live good lives. Just pause to think of the alternative: that we live our lives in blissful ignorance of the pain and suffering, the abuse and shame that our Christian brothers and sisters are causing or we just let it ride even though we are aware of it—and they do the same with us. All too often this is pastoral reality, but it should not be, not least in a church that across continents has allowed the abuse of children to go unchecked. Jesus' language is graphic and shocking precisely because Jesus wants us to understand just how important it is to him that we show each other and ourselves respect in this way.

Caring for those God cares for

> Make sure that you do not look down on one of these little ones. For I tell you that their angels in heaven continually see the face of my heavenly Father. 12 What do you reckon? If a man had one hundred sheep and one of them was led astray, would he not leave the ninety-nine on the hills and go to look for the one being led astray? 13 And if he happens to find it, I tell you straight, he rejoices over it more than over the other ninety-nine that had not been

---

his expectation that his body will be fully restored at the resurrection (2 Macc 7:11). For further discussion of the resurrection of the dead in Second Temple Judaism and early Christianity, see Wright, *Resurrection*. For further comment on Jesus exaggerating to drive the point home, see Davies and Allison, *Matthew*, 1:525 and *Matthew*, 2:766.

led astray. 14 Likewise, it is not the will of your heavenly Father that any one of these little ones should perish. (Matt 18:10–14)[17]

In order to underline his point, Jesus tells a parable with the punchline that God the Father does not want any of Jesus' disciples to fall into sin, fall away from faith and following him, and end up in eternal punishment. The idea that God does not want to punish his people is not new, the very same idea can be found in Lamentations 3:31–33. God is just and will mete out justice, including punishment on those who do wrong; God also shows compassionate love to his people and so longs for them to repent so he might forgive them. Jesus stresses the compassionate love of his heavenly Father and the Father's desire that all his disciples might gain eternal life.

The life of discipleship is not all plain sailing. Temptations come and stumbling into sin is an ever-present possibility. God the Father does not want this for Jesus' disciples. So, he acts like the shepherd in the parable. The angels who care for Jesus' disciples are continually before God in the throne room of heaven (worshipping and ready to be sent by God to do whatever he commands).[18] God sees both them and the disciples they represent. Just as the shepherd leaves the flock to seek the one lost sheep, so God seeks out the disciple who is lost. Just as the shepherd rejoices over the lost sheep when he finds it, so God celebrates restoring the disciple who has fallen away and been brought back because he does not want even one of Jesus' disciples to go astray into a life of sin and so forfeit eternal life.

If God the Father does not want any of Jesus' disciples to be lost to sin and eternal punishment, then why should any of Jesus' disciples act as if they did not particularly care about this possibility? Jesus highlights the love, grace, and forgiveness of the Father, and the energy he puts into seeking out the lost, in order to encourage all his disciples to look out for one another. "Make sure that you do not look down on one of these little ones." Looking down on, despising, scorning, or in any other way belittling fellow disciples when they fall into any kind of sin not only does not help them but constitutes acting in exactly the opposite way to God—and is therefore itself a serious sin. Jesus teaches his disciples to treat each other differently,

---

17. Some manuscripts have v. 11 "for the Son of Man came to (seek and) save the lost." It is missing in several of the most important witnesses. It is easier to explain this fact on the basis that it was added later. See, e.g., France, *Matthew*, 684.

18. On angels being ready to do God's bidding, see Angel, *Angels*, 30–42. On whether these angels are guardian angels or whether they are the group of angels looking after the people of God, see ibid., 75–82.

to care for each other when we get things wrong in just the same way as God treats us.

Handling conflicts

> If your Christian brother [or sister] sins against you, go and help them to see it, just you and them on your own. If they listen to you, you have regained your Christian brother [or sister]. 16 But if they do not listen, take with you one or two others, so that "every word should be confirmed by one or two witnesses." 17 But if they pay no attention to them, talk to the church. But if they pay no attention to the church, let them be to you [individually] like the gentile and the tax collector. 18 I tell you honestly, whatever you bind on earth will be bound in heaven, and whatever you loose on earth will be loosed in heaven. 19 Again I tell you honestly, if two of you agree on earth about some matter about which you are asking, it will be done for you by my Father in heaven. 20 For where two or three are gathering in my name, there I am in the middle of them. (Matt 18:15–20)

Context is everything, particularly here. Outside of its current context, these verses might read as an accountability structure that could quite easily err into a culture of bullying. Find the accused, force them into confession, and if they have the integrity to refuse to admit to something they have not done, then take them up through the various stages of the disciplinary process until you reach expulsion from the company or community. However, after vv. 10–14, such a reading is simply not possible. Having exhorted his disciples to follow the example of God the Father to seek out and save those who are wandering off into sin, Jesus can hardly be instructing them in the immediately following verses to throw them out of fellowship on the basis of a few interviews with no attempt to help them.

The context for Jesus' instruction in vv. 15–18 is his teaching in vv. 1–14 and in vv. 21–35. Christian disciples are to be humble before each other. We are not to attempt to exercise power or control over each other but are to become disarmingly powerless and transparent with one another. We are to accept each other. We are to seek to be holy ourselves and root out from our lives the things that draw us back into sinful ways of behaving. We are to recognize that the world will be full of temptations but we are not to succumb to them or add to them. We are to be really careful to make sure that the way we behave does not cause anyone else to fall into sin. We are to look out for our Christian brothers and sisters and help them if they fall into sin, just as God seeks us out and helps us when we wander off. We are to forgive each other just as God has forgiven us and continues to forgive us.

Discipline looks and feels very different, depending on the way it is done and the attitudes that people bring to it. When Christian disciples bring the following attitudes to following Jesus' instructions in vv. 15–18, then it looks and feels much more like the restoration of relationship between people who love each other, which is precisely what Jesus instructs us to make church discipline. The very fact that this is a stepped process reveals the grace at the heart of it. Speaking alone together first of all gives an opportunity to sort out the issues without bringing any more public shame into the situation. It gives the opportunity to diffuse the situation. Speaking in the first place gives the opportunity to sort the situation out rather than letting the structures of injustice creep into the life of the community or giving cause for resentment and lingering anger.

When Jesus instructs the brother or sister who has been sinned against to take two or three people with them as a second step towards reconciliation, he quotes the Old Testament so that "every word should be confirmed by one or two witnesses" (Deut 19:15). The idea behind having two or three witnesses is to make sure that the truth is being told so that there is no injustice done. The passage in Deuteronomy continues with process for dealing with false witnesses so that people are discouraged from making malicious and false accusations (Deut 19:16–21). Far from being a mechanism for bullying, Jesus intends his disciples to ensure that their mutual discipline is based in truth-telling and fairness. He builds accountability into the system to ensure this happens, and to make sure that all parties are treated fairly and honestly.

The final step is to take the matter to the church congregation, and the idea behind this remains the attempt to bring about reconciliation.[19] The disciplinary measure feels severe. If the brother or sister remains unrepentant for the sin they have committed, they are to be treated as "the gentile or the tax collector"—which has suggested to many interpreters, exclusion from the church community.[20] However, a small detail in the text suggests that this may not be Jesus' focus. Jesus says "let them be *to you personally* (singular)...," not "let them be to the church community...." This suggests

---

19. Davies and Allison, *Matthew*, 2:785 (not the universal church).
20. Davies and Allison, *Matthew*, 2:785; Luz, *Matthew 8–20*, 452.

that the relationship breakdown and discipline is limited to the two parties. Moreover, a sting of grace lies in the tail of this instruction. Jesus cannot intend this to mean the permanent and irreversible relationship breakdown or exclusion of the unrepentant brother or sister, because his own treatment of tax collectors and gentiles (and the way he commands others to treat them) is quite the opposite of permanent and irreversible relationship breakdown and exclusion from his community of disciples. Jesus uses the gentiles as examples of people who lead unholy lives (Matt 5:47; 6:7, 32: 20:25), but he also commands his disciples to make disciples of them (Matt 28:18–20) in fulfillment of prophecy (Matt 12:18–21).[21] Jesus does speak of tax collectors as sinners (Matt 5:46; 9:10), but he calls them to follow him (Matt 9:9, 11; 11:19) and shows confidence that those who do will enter the kingdom of heaven (Matt 21:31–32). On the lips of Jesus, gentiles and tax collectors are not irredeemable sinners. They are people who have sinned and turned their backs on God. Therefore, they are people to bring to the repentance and obedience of true discipleship. Church discipline ought not to be anything more that recognizing where people stand before God and each other and living honestly in the light of that self-recognition. However, that can be costly and difficult where we refuse to recognize our sinfulness and admit to it to each other.

Jesus teaches that the decisions the church makes about formally recognizing relationship breakdown between members are ratified in heaven, "whatever you bind on earth will be bound in heaven," as are their decisions about restoring members to fellowship with each other, "whatever you loose on earth will be loosed in heaven."[22] In this context, he adds that whatever two of his disciples agree upon and ask for, his heavenly Father will establish. The reason Jesus gives for this is that wherever two or three of his disciples are gathered in his name, he is present with them. Jesus promises to be present in the difficult activities of honest and open conversations about sinning against and hurting each other, and about trying to talk through issues until justice and reconciliation are reached. He is also present in the discipline of an unrepentant sinner, and in the church loving

---

21. Matthew uses two different but related words for "gentile," *ethnos* and *ethnikos*. I can see no reason for distinguishing sharply in meaning between them—and no reason is suggested by either Davies and Allison (*Matthew*, 2:785) or Luz (*Matthew 8–20*, 452–53).

22. Luz, *Matthew 8–20*, 452–53, especially n.37, where he notes that already by the time of the Didache exclusion from fellowship lasts only until the sinner repents (Did. 15.3).

the unrepentant brother or sister and seeking their restoration to fellowship. Jesus promises to be present in the pain of his church.

None of this should come as any surprise. Teaching and learning holiness is a messy business. We do not learn holiness all at once. We make mistakes. We hurt God, each other, and ourselves. We need to find the space to repent and apologize, to offer and receive forgiveness. If Jesus had commanded his disciples to make disciples of all nations, teaching them to obey all he had commanded them, without having a plan for when his disciples messed things up, his mission action plan would have been lacking in (at least) one very important respect. But again, there is hope in all this because Jesus does not abandon his disciples to sorting out their own failures, relationship breakdown, and arguments. Jesus promises to be present with his disciples in the difficult aspects of their relationships, as we learn to love each other in all our dysfunctionality, as we fail to love each other, and, after trust and friendship have been lost, as we learn to build up relationships of love and honesty again.

Jesus' promise to be present amongst his disciples in all this is one of three promises of his presence in the Gospel (Matt 2:23; 18:20; 28:20). In each, Jesus is identified as God. Jesus will be called Emmanuel, "God with us" (Matt 2:23). Here Jesus' statement about being present amongst two or three gathered in his name recalls rabbinic sayings about the glorious presence of God amongst two or three studying the Torah (Matt 18:20; m. 'Abot 3:2–3).[23] When he promises his presence to his disciples until the end of the ages he does so as the heavenly Son of Man and the Son into whose name disciples are baptized (Matt 28:16–20). In each of these promises, Jesus is the God who saves his people from their sins. He will be called Emmanuel because he will save his people from their sins (Matt 2:23). In baptism Jesus forgives sins and in teaching disciples to obey his commandments, Jesus helps his disciples to live righteously and avoid sin (Matt 28:19–20). In the process of restoring relationships after break down, in discipline and restoration of relationships after discipline, Jesus is present helping his disciples to work through very practical issues of what love really entails at the sharp end (Matt 18:15–20). In teaching us how to live and taking us through the restoration of broken relationships, Jesus teaches his disciples what forgiveness really means.

23. Davies and Allison, *Matthew*, 2:789–90. The relevant lines are "but two who are sitting, and the words of the Torah do pass between them—the Presence is with them" (m. 'Abot 3:2) and "but three who ate at a single table and did talk about teachings of the Torah while at that table are as if they ate at the table of the Omnipresent" (m. 'Abot 3:3).

Five (Dirty) Words Every Christian Needs to Learn

Forgiveness

> Then Peter came to him and said, "Lord, how many times if my fellow disciple sins against me, should I forgive them? As many as seven times?" 22 Jesus said to him, "I tell you, not as many as seven times but as many as seventy times seven." 23 On account of this, the kingdom of heaven may be likened to a man, a king, who wanted to settle accounts with his slaves. 24 When he began to settle accounts, one debtor who owed him ten thousand talents was brought to him. 25 But as he did not have the money to repay him, the master ordered him to be sold along with his wife, his children and everything he had, and the proceeds to go against the debt. 26 So, the slave fell down on the ground before him, begging him, "Be patient with me, and I will repay you every last penny." 27 Feeling gutted for this slave, the master released him and wiped out the debt. 28 This slave went off and found one of his fellow slaves who owed him one hundred denarii. He seized him and strangled him muttering, "Give me what you owe me." 29 So his fellow slave fell down and begged him, "Be patient with me and I will repay you every last penny." 30 But he did not want to, so he went off and threw him into prison until he should pay back what he owed. 31 So seeing all the goings on, his fellow slaves were extremely cut up and went off to report to their master everything that had gone on. 32 Then his master called him and said, "You evil slave, I wiped out that huge debt because you begged me. Shouldn't you have shown mercy to your fellow slave just as I showed mercy to you?" 34 And his master was furious and handed him over to the jailers until he should pay back every last penny he owed. 35 So my heavenly Father will do to you, if each one of you does not forgive your fellow disciples in your hearts and minds.[24] (Matt 18:21–35)

Peter finds this all rather challenging. Note that his difficulty is not how many times he should ask his brother or sister to repent for hurting him, or how many times he should be part of the church disciplining an unrepentant Christian brother or sister. He does not express any difficulty with disciplining a fellow follower of Jesus. His problem concerns the question of how many times he might have to forgive someone. Imagine he talks to someone about their hurting him and they say sorry, and they mean it. But they have genuine difficulties. They do it again or they do something else to hurt him. He speaks to them and they ask forgiveness again. And it happens again, and again, and again. Peter wants to know where he can draw

---

24. Again, I translate with a little color at points as the parable is such a colorful one.

the line. Presumably, there comes a point where forgiveness simply has to be withheld?

Basically, Jesus says "No." There is no such line that his disciples can draw. By his response, Jesus has not drawn the line at 490 times (or seventy-seven times).[25] His "seventy times seven" means "you carry on forgiving when your Christian brother and sister repent."[26] The point of the parable is simple. God has forgiven us a debt far greater than we could ever forgive our fellow Christian. The things they do against us, however awful, cannot compare to the things we have done to God. We have all sought and received forgiveness from God. Therefore, we have no moral or spiritual right to withhold forgiveness from any brother or sister who honestly confesses their sin and asks forgiveness.

Jesus' final line "so will my heavenly Father do to you, if each one of you does not forgive your fellow disciples in your hearts and minds" adds nothing new to his message and cannot be ignored as a marginal threat that inhabits the fringes of the gospel of forgiveness. Jesus' own commentary on the prayer he taught us is "for if you do forgive people their trespasses, your heavenly Father will forgive you; but if you do not forgive other people, neither will your heavenly Father forgive your trespasses" (Matt 6:14–15). Forgiveness matters. Forgiveness matters to God and it ought to matter to us. God does not want solely to forgive us our sins so that we individually can enter his kingdom. God has a much bigger vision than this. God wants the whole world to repent of its sin so that all can be forgiven, and God wants the whole world to confess their sins to one another so that all can forgive each other. God wants total forgiveness and total restoration of relationship. For this, we all need to forgive each other as well as receive God's forgiveness. God calls the church to model his big vision to the world. When and where we do this, we live out his calling on our life together and help others to see who God truly is. And the beauty of this vision is that in it all, Jesus is present helping us to fulfill it every step of the way, all day, every day.

Perhaps Jesus' vision is not so bad after all. His focus on judgment is about the establishment of justice. His mission to make disciples is to bring the reality of that justice into the present world as well as the world to come.

25. There is a dispute about the best way to translate the number. For arguments for both sides, see Davies and Allison, *Matthew*, 2:793, where they comment aptly, "there is no need to resolve the issue, for both numbers amount to the same thing. One is not being commanded to count but to forgive without counting."

26. Davies and Allison, *Matthew*, 2:793.

His baptism in the name of Father, Son, and Holy Spirit is to bring forgiveness to those of us whose sins have alienated us from God and from others. His teaching us to obey his commands is about teaching us the right way to live lives of love. His community learning project puts forgiveness and respect for all right at the heart of the program. He calls all his followers to treat each other with love and respect, so we should sort out our issues as and when they arise. He instructs us to look out for each other, to support rather than judge each other, to work through our issues rather than ignore them, to love as he loves us, and to help each other in our struggles and wanderings away from lives of obedience to Jesus. He calls us to forgive each other just as he has forgiven us. In short, he calls us into authentic relationships of love. Yes, we give up our autonomy to obey a loving God. Yes, we live in obedience to his righteous commands rather than choosing our own way. Yes, we live in the humility that the knowledge that we will all stand before his throne of judgment and grace brings. But, then again, surely a humble church, whose members sought daily how we could live constructively to help each other out of sin as we all follow Jesus together, would not be such a bad thing?

6

Riding the Elephant

In the light of all this, ignoring the elephant under the carpet does not seem sensible. The elephant exists and we only live in denial of reality if we ignore it. Jesus did preach that we will all be held accountable for our wrongdoings. Jesus did teach that there would be a day of judgment. Jesus did not advise us to ignore this because some kind of morally insipid love (that does not take the damage we do to ourselves and others seriously) will triumph over justice by ignoring it. Nor did he teach that we can avoid being held accountable through faith in such love. Jesus calls us all to repent of our wrongdoings and follow him. He teaches us to obey his commandments and live lives of holiness in his community of disciples, humbly helping each other to grow in righteousness where we have our own lives sorted and so the moral right to do so. He did not break the law or teach breaking the law—and he certainly did not do so in the name of love. He taught that loving God and neighbor was the highpoint of the law and all his commandments make sense in the light of these two most important commands. We are to obey all that Jesus commanded but we need not be afraid of this as too tall an order because Jesus promises that he himself will be present with us all day every day teaching us how to live—and he commits to doing this in humility, kindness, and gentleness, as well as with the strength to see us through. This being the elephant under the carpet, we ought not to ignore it but learn to ride it.

Reflections

I think the problem with too much Christianity I encounter today is that we replace the person of Jesus with a doctrine of grace. Faith starts with acknowledging and receiving Jesus Christ as our Savior, Lord, and the Way, the Truth, and the Life. It begins as we repent of our sins and commit to following him. As we accept him as Savior, we receive his forgiveness and lose our shame and guilt. This loss of shame and guilt can be a very powerful experience and in itself can be life-changing. Listening to others describing their experience of forgiveness and leaving their shame and guilt behind can be profoundly moving. I suspect that it is the very power of these experiences that leads us to focus on this aspect of our acceptance by Jesus so heavily. Sometimes we can concentrate on it almost to the exclusion of other aspects of our accepting him. We can so fall in love with grace that we begin to forget to love Jesus.

When we do this, we do not meet the living Lord but only one part of his CV. Rather than meeting Jesus in person as we worship, pray, and follow him in humble obedience, we seek that part of his story that meets our perceived needs. We want acceptance, and the kind of love that does not question who we are but receives us as who we are. We like the aspects of the cross that deal with the barrier between us and God, as we want the barrier taken down. We like the idea of unconditional love because it gives us the sense of self-worth that we all need and some of us crave. And many pastors and teachers preach this message:

> All the pardon, the approval, the purpose, the freedom, the rescue, the meaning, the righteousness, the cleansing, the significance, the worth and the affection we crave and need are already ours in Christ. We don't need to add anything to it. The operative power that makes you a Christian is the same operative power that keeps you a Christian: the unconditional, unqualified, undeserved, unrestrained grace of God in the completed work of Christ.[1]

---

1. Tchividjian, *Jesus*, 205–6. To be fair, he does struggle with where following Jesus and obedience fit with his understanding of grace on pp. 187–88 and I really like the honesty of the book. I also think his purpose is to win people over to following Jesus. My difficulty with the book is that it avoids all Jesus' talk of judgment and accountability in order to play up the love of Christ. My point is that we do not need to be afraid of Jesus' judgment because *he* prepares us for that day. We just need to invite him in daily to do his work of making us more like himself. There is no need to take refuge from Jesus in our "bigging up" the doctrine of grace.

We do this because we think that the answer to our problems is someone who loves us for who we are, by which we mean someone who will not ask us to change.

As a result, we find the full picture of Jesus in the Gospels threatening. We edit out all his sayings about judgment or we find ways of assigning them to history. Those people in the past (normally the Pharisees) were whitewashed sepulchers, hypocrites, faithless and unbelieving sinners. We acknowledge that his twelve disciples could sometimes show little faith, but we seem less ready to think about *ourselves* in these terms. We are forgiven, accepted, loved, and free. Where Jesus talks of obedience to his commands, we find his words puzzling and sometimes a bit disturbing, but normally there is someone on hand to reassure us (normally from bits of Paul) that we are saved and we do not need to worry. So, we edit Jesus out of his own story.

We read the Gospels for the message we want to hear—that we are accepted and acceptable, and God loves us. In our minds and hearts, we turn reading the Gospels into a scrapbooking exercise. We cut out the stories we love and the ones we can interpret to give us the message we want to hear, and we give them pride of place in our spiritual scrapbooks. We do the same with the teaching of Jesus. We tend to cut out the sayings about judgment and the parts of his teaching we find too challenging or inconvenient for the way we want to live our lives. We color round the stories and sayings we enjoy and make them the focal point of our spirituality. When we are done with editing the Gospels, we take our scrapbooks and make them our Bibles, leaving the rest of the Gospel stories behind. Instead of reading the Gospels to learn Jesus and listen to his teaching, we diminish Jesus by creating our own picture of him—one that meets our perceived emotional needs. We find all sorts of ways of doing this and generally ones that fit our church traditions. (I have seen this process in evangelical and liberal traditions, in high and low churches, in open and conservative churches, and in every spirituality that I have come across, from Celtic to charismatic.) Once we are done, we have a Jesus of our own making.

On paper, this Jesus saves us. We think, believe, and/or feel that this Jesus does what we want our faith or spirituality to do. We desire acceptance and this seems to give us acceptance. Behind all this we desire legitimation—the knowledge and sense that somehow, somewhere, someone can say for sure that nobody has the right to criticize us and that we are okay. We confuse this desire of contemporary Western culture with the salvation that Jesus offers. This is tragic because in doing this, we simply make our "faith" mirror a current social trend. During the course of the twentieth century, much of liberal Western society has become so focused on self-worth and rights that it has forgotten duties.[2] Societies suffer as a result because people are happy to claim what they want but are less happy to contribute. We want more from the common good than we are prepared to put into it, as we focus on our own needs and self-worth rather than those of our neighbors. Seeking responsibility-free spirituality where God meets our perceived needs and we have no obligation to obey his commands is simply a spiritualization of this trend in society. Of course, there would be nothing wrong with this *if* this is what Jesus taught. But he did not. He taught love *and judgment*, forgiveness *and obedience*. So, we become spiritually unhealthy and unproductive when we fixate on our acceptance by God and get stuck in that one part of the story. We replace the living Lord with a doctrine of grace of our own making, and so cut ourselves off from the living Lord.

Unsurprisingly, some Christians get bored. For those of us who have got bored, our boredom should not come as a shock. If we insist on getting off the bus, we cannot complain if it leaves the stop without us. If we choose to stick our spiritual scrapbook over the face of the living Lord Jesus and get stuck at one point in the story (which was never intended as the final destination), then we cannot complain if we find our spiritual experience unfulfilling.

There are two pieces of good news for those of us who have made this mistake. First, Jesus never intended that this should be the life or journey of any of his disciples. He intended the repentance, forgiveness, and acceptance to lead into a restored relationship with God in which God teaches each of us personally how to live in holiness and love. That remains a lifelong challenge for most of us, and one that does not lead to boredom. At least, I have yet to meet the holy and loving person who is bored with God. Second, Jesus knows we make mistakes and this side of judgment day waits patiently for us to come back to him as gentle teacher and living Lord. Jesus wants to rescue us from the false doctrines of grace we make for ourselves. Jesus wants to restore us to a loving and learning relationship with him as Savior, Lord, and teacher. It all starts with repentance and acceptance of Christ as Lord.

---

2. This is at the heart of the thesis of David Selbourne's *The Principle of Duty*.

The Jesus You *Really* Didn't Know

Rediscovering Jesus the teacher

None of this is new. As a kid I went to Sunday school and holiday clubs. We sang some old songs there. The churches that did the holiday clubs did not seem to have updated their song lists since the 1930s. When I was a little bit older, I became a cathedral chorister. The music cupboards were stuffed full of music written in the sixteenth century. I am grateful for all the old music I learned as a kid, because it spoke of the risen Christ of the Gospels teaching me his way and the work of the Holy Spirit making me more like Jesus.

> He lives, he lives, Christ Jesus lives today
> He walks with me and he talks with me along life's narrow way
> He lives, he lives, salvation to impart,
> You ask me how I know he lives? He lives within my heart.

Look it up and read the rest of the hymn. I am guessing that Alfred Henry Ackley (1887–1960) understood that Christian discipleship involved following Jesus daily. He seems to have been grateful for the victory won on the cross that means that he was accepted by God *and* he seems to have understood that this means walking daily with the risen Christ in service of him. Another old hymn (written slightly earlier) spells it out even more clearly.

> When we walk with the Lord
> In the light of his Word,
> What a glory he sheds on our way;
> While we do his good will,
> He abides with us still,
> And with all who will trust and obey.

John H. Sammis' (1846–1919) famous chorus to this hymn exhorts us all to trust and obey because there is no other way to be happy in Jesus. I am going to hazard another guess that he too not only understood but experienced in his life what it meant to live with Jesus as our teacher, and to find the great gain of godliness with contentment. My personal favorite, however, has to be the following, which I reckon to be the best song or hymn ever written to call the Holy Spirit into our lives to transform us into the people God would have us be.

> Come down, O love divine, seek Thou this soul of mine,
> And visit it with Thine own ardor glowing.
> O Comforter, draw near, within my heart appear,
> And kindle it, Thy holy flame bestowing.

O let it freely burn, 'til earthly passions turn
To dust and ashes in its heat consuming;
And let Thy glorious light shine ever on my sight,
And clothe me round, the while my path illuming.

Let holy charity mine outward vesture be,
And lowliness become mine inner clothing;
True lowliness of heart, which takes the humbler part,
And o'er its own shortcomings weeps with loathing.

And so the yearning strong, with which the soul will long,
Shall far outpass the power of human telling;
For none can guess its grace, till he become the place
Wherein the Holy Spirit makes His dwelling.

Bianco da Siena (died 1434) invites the Holy Spirit into his life to burn away all sinful passions and clothe him in love and humility. He prays for the kind of humility that not only recognizes sin but regrets it, and for the yearning that desires more of God's work of holiness in his life. The last two lines suggest to me that he knew that we only get how wonderful and desirable this grace of holiness is when the Holy Spirit, living within us, does this work.

These are just three songs. There are plenty more. Isaac Watts (1674–1748) wrote, "He turns our feet from sinful ways and pardons what our hands have done." Charles Wesley (1757–1834) prayed, "Jesus confirm my heart's desire to work, and speak, and think for Thee." Even contemporary song writers (despite their tendency to focus on the presence and love of God) sometimes pen lyrics which ask God to teach us obedience. Christian hymnody down the ages and into the present-day bears witness to the fact that Christians have known the presence of the Lord Jesus Christ in their lives as their gentle and humble teacher, picking them up when they stumble and teaching them how to live the life of righteousness to which each one of us is called. What is more, the hymn writers celebrate this work and invite Jesus to do more of it in their lives. If I understand their hymns at all, they had (and have) discovered Jesus as their teacher.

Not only is none of this new but it is so much better that putting our faith in a doctrine of grace (and so making an idol of it). A doctrine has no power to save us, no acceptance to offer us, and no love to share with us. The living Lord Jesus has all these things and he wants to save, accept, and love us. He also wants to save us and others from the damage our sinfulness does, and so he wants to teach us how to live. What is more, if we follow

Jesus daily in humility and obedience, in prayer and worship, in love and in grace, we have nothing to fear from the God of judgment. Jesus is this God who will come again to judge the living and the dead. It is this same Jesus who promises to come alongside us and prepare us for that day, forgiving our sins and patiently teaching us how to live out his commands so that we can truly love God with all our soul, heart, mind, and strength, and love our friends and enemies as we love ourselves. *Jesus loves us*. He died so that on that day he could say to us "Well done, my good and faithful servant" rather than "I never knew you, depart from me you workers of lawlessness."

In the vivid picture Jesus paints of his coming to judge the nations, both the righteous and the wicked call Jesus "Lord" (Matt 25:37, 44). However, it is only those who have lived in obedience to Jesus' commands whom he welcomes into the kingdom of heaven. When the rich young man heard that following Jesus meant giving away his possessions, he found the challenge profoundly difficult (Matt 19:22). In the face of Jesus' teaching, we too can find some of the challenges of discipleship hard. On the day he spoke with that young man, the disciples suggested that it was impossible for anyone to be saved (Matt 19:25). Jesus made a memorable reply: "For people this is impossible, but for God all things are possible" (Matt 19:26). I suspect that Jesus was not only talking about his dying on the cross to forgive us our sins but that he was also talking about his ministry amongst us teaching us to keep his commands and so saving us (and others) from ourselves (and our sinfulness). Like that young man, we may believe that we cannot change our ways because we are too addicted to our lifestyles and choices. We need to believe that God can really change us, that Jesus can come alongside us each day and in humility and gentleness teach us how to live out his commands—because he can. If we want to worship Jesus Christ as Lord, we need to meet him as teacher, because he alone has the power to help us put meaning into the word "Lord"—and nothing is impossible with God.

Appendix

Thoughts on Jesus, Paul, and the Law

A key question hanging around after all I have written above is, which commands of the Torah still ought to be obeyed? Does Jesus really think it is an abomination if we eat ostrich meat (Lev 11:16)? Traditionally the Christian church has not observed every command in Torah. Gentile Christians eat pork (Lev 11:7). The question of which commands in the Torah still apply has been discussed by Christians throughout the history of the church. I have argued that Jesus teaches his disciples to teach obedience to everything that he has commanded, not a stripped-down version of his teaching that cuts out some or all of his commands. Given Jesus' words "teaching them to obey *all* the things I have commanded you" (Matt 28:20) and "if you love me, you will keep my commandments" (John 14:15), it contradicts any plain reading of the text to argue that the Jesus of the canonical Gospels expected anything less of his disciples. To do so involves pretending either that Jesus did not say these words or that he did not really mean them. I prefer to take Jesus' words seriously and am urging my Christian brothers and sisters to do the same.

I have argued in some detail against a view that seems to be prevalent in many churches today: that the only two commandments we have to take seriously are to love God and love our neighbor, and that it is up to us to work out how this looks in practice. This does not reflect the teaching of Jesus as presented in the Gospel of Matthew. I would go further and state that this does not reflect the teaching of Jesus in Mark, Luke, or John either —although I have not tried to demonstrate that in detail here. Nor does it

Appendix

reflect the teaching of Paul, who very clearly spent many a pastoral hour trying to encourage the members of his churches to grow in holiness and obedience to the form of teaching to which they had been entrusted (Rom 6:17). Rather, Jesus taught and teaches his disciples to live in obedience to all his commands.

This raises a thorny issue: what do we make of Jesus' saying, "Honestly, I tell you, until heaven and earth pass away not one of the tiniest bits of punctuation will drop off the page of the law, until all things are accomplished" (Matt 5:18)? I have given my basic answer to the question in chapter 2: we follow the commands of Jesus. Jesus made an unusual and (it seems) unique theological move. He spoke of *his* law. He instructed his disciples "take *my yoke* upon you" (Matt 11:29). The "yoke" was a rabbinic metaphor for the law. No other rabbi seems ever to have spoken of *their* yoke.[1] There would have been good reason for this. *God* gave the law. It was *God's* law and not the law of any particular rabbi. Yet Jesus did speak of his yoke, of his law. He also stated that he was the one true teacher of the law (Matt 23:8). Jesus claimed both the right to give the final interpretation of the law and the right to talk of it as his law. In doing this, Jesus identifies himself with God because he has taken on the role of God.[2] He has also given the law a new identity and boundaries. He identifies his interpretation of the law so closely with the law that *for Jesus, the law is now his interpretation of the law, and nothing else*. As followers of Jesus, Christians have committed themselves to living according to his teachings.

But the question of how we understand Jesus' theology here (at least as Matthew presents it) remains for those of us who puzzle over these things. Jesus teaches that we should obey all the things he has commanded. Fine—although we can find this difficult in practice at times. But Paul does seem to have had a problem with this. How do we square Jesus' teaching that not the slightest thing will pass from the law until all things are accomplished (Matt 5:18) with Paul scolding the Galatian Christians for trying to do the works of the law (Gal 3:2) and telling them that no one is justified by the law (Gal 3:11)? Surely Paul preaches that we are now free from the law? So, why should we talk of obeying commands? The question is not new, and down the centuries Christian thinkers and teachers have given answers. Below, I will give you a brief overview of my own answer to this question—but

---

1. Davies and Allison, *Matthew*, 2:289.

2. For an exploration of Jesus' divine identity, see Bauckham, *Jesus and the God of Israel*.

with the caveat that I am still thinking it through and would like to return to it again one day, and perhaps write something on it. I would also like to point out that not having the perfect answer to the question does not invalidate the main argument of this book. Jesus' teaching, as the Gospels present it, remains authoritative for every Christian who takes their faith seriously, regardless of how convincing (or otherwise) my current answer to the questions surrounding Jesus, Paul, and the law may be.

In short, I believe the answer to the question to be that Jesus was preaching the gospel to the Jews and Paul was preaching the gospel to the gentiles. The Jews already had the covenants and promises and were facing a coming judgment in the destruction of the temple, which Jesus prophesied. Jesus called them to repent of their sins and live in obedience to the law until the destruction of the temple, after which event they were bound only to obey his teachings. Paul proclaimed the gospel to the gentiles as if the destruction of the temple had already happened. They were now the temple (and body of Christ, the new temple) where others would meet God. So, they were not bound to obey all the commandments in the Torah but only the teachings of Jesus. The clash over the law between the Jewish Christians and Paul happened because the temple had not yet been destroyed. So, Christians in Jerusalem and Judea were bound to obey the whole Torah whereas the gentile Christians were bound only to obey the teachings of Jesus. Some of the Christians in Jerusalem were not quite sure the gentile converts had quite got the right idea and so tried to convert them to obedience to the whole Torah. This caused the clash. However, neither group for one minute would imagine that the teachings of Jesus were optional. I will flesh out this idea below in five steps.

Step one: Jesus taught *Jews* obedience to Torah *until* heaven and earth pass away

The Gospel of Matthew places the following words on Jesus' lips: "Do not say to yourselves that I have come to destroy the law or the prophets: I have not come to destroy them but to fulfill them. 18 Honestly, I tell you, *until heaven and earth pass away* not one of the tiniest bits of punctuation will drop off the page of the law, until all things are accomplished" (Matt 5:18). The Gospel of Luke records a similar saying of Jesus: ". . . but it is easier for heaven and earth to pass away than for one tiny bit of punctuation to drop

Appendix

from the law" (Luke 16:17). These two sayings are not identical and should not be pressed into saying the same thing. However, both clearly talk about changing anything in the law in terms of heaven and earth disappearing. Therefore, they both suggest that even the tiniest changes in the law are quite momentous.

Luke talks about such changes in terms of their being easier than heaven and earth disappearing, so suggesting that changes in the law are extraordinary events that are momentously difficult to establish. Matthew makes a more precise statement. He states that nothing in the law will disappear until (or except that) heaven and earth disappear. This would suggest that if heaven and earth disappeared, things in the law might go with them. This puts Jesus' following statement about obedience to commands into an interesting context: "Therefore, whoever loosens up one of the least of these commands and teaches other people to do the same will be called least in the kingdom of heaven. Whoever does them and teaches them, these people will be called great in the kingdom of heaven" (Matt 5:19). Should heaven and earth pass away, then the commands may well be loosened up because Jesus has noted the possibility of this happening in the previous verse.

Step two: Jesus taught Jews that heaven and earth would pass away when the temple was destroyed, and parts of the Torah would disappear at this time

(This may be the most controversial step in the argument.) Towards the end of his earthly ministry, Matthew, Mark, and Luke all record Jesus talking to his disciples about trials, tribulations, and the coming of the Son of Man. In all three Gospels, the conversation begins with the disciples noting the beauty of the temple in Jerusalem (Matt 24:1; Mark 13:1; Luke 21:5). Jesus predicts that it will be destroyed (Matt 24:2; Mark 13:2; Luke 21:6). The disciples ask when this will happen (Matt 24:3; Mark 13:4; Luke 21:7). Jesus responds (Matt 24:4–44; Mark 13:5–37; Luke 21:8–36). However, interpreters of the Gospels are not entirely agreed whether or where Jesus answers the question.[3]

---

3. The "Son of Man problem" (so called) is so convoluted that I am not going to attempt to note the relevant literature, as it is vast. Instead, I will note one book that gathers together some of the more important writings in the subject: Reynolds, *Son of Man Problem*. Interested readers can start there and gradually work their way through the

Possibly, Jesus changes subject to talk about the end times.[4] Maybe Jesus does answer the question in his comment about the abomination of desolation (Matt 24:15; Mark 13:14).[5] Or it might be that Jesus thought that the temple would be destroyed when the Son of Man came.[6] I have already made quite a detailed case for what I think elsewhere so will offer only the briefest sketch here.[7] I prefer to assume that Jesus spoke coherently and that the Gospel writers edited coherently. Therefore, I assume that Jesus did answer the disciples' question about when the temple would be destroyed. So, I prefer not to suggest that Jesus simply changed the subject from the temple to the end times unless there is no alternative explanation.

I also cannot agree that the statement about the abomination of desolation refers to the destruction of the temple. The phrase "abomination of desolation" is borrowed from the book of Daniel where it is used to refer to a pagan altar being set up on top of the altar of burnt offering in the Jerusalem temple (Dan 9:25; 11:31; 12:11; see 1 Macc 1:54 for the full story). The altar of burnt offering stood in the temple and so the "abomination of desolation" must have been built on top of it within the temple. Matthew and Mark report Jesus using a phrase that evokes something extremely unclean happening within the temple, not the destruction of the temple. This suggests that Matthew and Mark see the temple still standing at this point in Jesus' prophecy. Moreover, although Luke does not refer to the "abomination of desolation," at this point in his report of the prophecy, he has "when you see Jerusalem surrounded by enemy camps, then know that its desolation has come near" (Luke 21:20). This too implies that the temple is still standing at this point in Jesus' prophecy.

---

select bibliography he provides. I will also recommend Robert H. Stein, *Jesus, the Temple and the Coming of the Son of Man* for its lucidity in taking the reader through the text and the issues. However, I think Stein misses some important aspects of the discussion and so comes to the wrong answer.

4. E.g., Hare, *Matthew*, 273–83.

5. E.g., Adams, *Stars Will fall*, 144. Adams provides a nuanced version of this argument: "[T]he expression itself [abomination of desolation], within this context, conveys a linkage between the occurrence/appearance of the 'abomination' and the temple's anticipated destruction." This may not equate the abomination exactly with the temple but it puts the two within the same sequence of events and timeframe. One might argue that this is compatible with reading the coming of the Son of Man as referring to the destruction of the temple, but I suspect that this is not what Adams intends his audience to hear.

6. E.g., Wright, *Victory of God*, 339–68.

7. Angel, *Chaos*.

Appendix

So, I opt for interpreting the coming of the Son of Man as the coming of Jesus as God in judgment on Jerusalem. The language of sun, moon, and stars falling from the sky was used metaphorically in the OT to refer to the judgment of God on nations in earth *within history*. It was also used this way by many Jews at the time of Jesus. Interestingly, Jesus quotes words about the sun, moon, and stars falling from the sky from prophecies about God punishing two wicked cities, Babylon and Edom (Isa 13:10; 34:4). This suggests that Jesus might also be talking about the punishment of a wicked city. Jesus also quotes the vision of "one like a son of man" coming into heaven (Dan 7:2–14) from Daniel, who interprets it as being about kingdoms *on earth* (Dan 7:17–18, 23–27). So, I cannot see why Jesus might not use the same language similarly. Many Jewish writers at the time of Jesus also used this language to describe judgment. Generally, the gentiles were identified as the wicked whom God would punish before he then re-established his people Israel in the land he had promised to Abraham. Jesus also uses this language to describe the judgment of God on a wicked nation and the destruction of their city. The only real difference between Jesus and his Jewish contemporaries is that he prophesies that the nation to be punished is Judea and the city to be destroyed is Jerusalem.[8] (Incidentally, I do think that Jesus speaks about the second coming, but in Matt 25:31–46, where the Son of Man clearly judges all the nations of the world.)

So, the language of sun, moon, and stars falling from heaven (Matt 24:29–31; Mark 13:24–27) and the language of signs in the heavens, chaos on earth, and the roaring of the seas (Luke 21:25) refers to the judgment of Judea and the destruction of Jerusalem and its temple. At the end of this prophecy, Matthew and Luke record Jesus giving a timeframe for this event and saying that although heaven and earth would pass away, his words would never pass away: "I tell you the truth, that this generation will not pass away until all these things have happened. Heaven and earth will pass away but my words will never pass away" (Matt 24:34–35); "I tell you the truth, that this generation will not pass away until everything has happened. Heaven and earth will pass away but my words will never pass away" (Luke 21:32–33). The timeframe Jesus gives for the coming of the Son of Man is before the generation listening to him passes away. That generation did not pass away before the temple was destroyed. This happened in AD 70. So in talking about the coming of the Son of Man and giving this timeframe, Jesus answers his disciples' question about when the temple

---

8. For a more detailed argument, see Angel, *Chaos*, 125–39.

would be destroyed. (For those who think the coming of the Son of Man in these texts was about something different from the judgment of God on Judea and the temple, there remains the very awkward issue of Jesus seeming to be wrong about the time of the second coming, which would then be problematic for Christian faith.)

So, Jesus answered the disciples' question using the apocalyptic language of his day. The temple would be destroyed when God punished the nation for its sinfulness by sending armies that would destroy Jerusalem. This would happen before the generation of his hearers died off. He uses language of heaven, earth, and sea being thrown into disorder to describe this event. He even talks of heaven and earth passing away (Matt 24:35; Luke 21:33). The only other place where Matthew and Luke talk of heaven and earth passing away is where he says that nothing will drop from the law until heaven and earth pass away (Matt 5:18; Luke 16:17). The alert reader of Matthew and Luke will pick that up and notice that when the temple is destroyed, heaven and earth pass away, which means that parts of the law may also disappear. Interestingly, when Jesus speaks of heaven and earth passing away he speaks of *his words* never passing away. In other words, parts of the Torah may pass away but none of Jesus' teaching will do so.

Putting step one and step two together, we reach the following conclusion: that Jesus taught that the temple would be destroyed within a generation, and that parts of the law would disappear with it. Until that time, his Jewish followers were to obey the whole law. After that time, they were only to obey his teachings, as they never pass away.

Step three: Paul taught gentiles that they were not under the law but that they were to obey Jesus' teaching

Paul certainly does say, "if you are led by the Spirit, you are not under law" (Gal 5:18). Out of context, this could easily be read to mean something like "as Christians with the Holy Spirit inside us we do not have to follow the law." Reading Paul this way poses problems. Paul says, "for the whole law is fulfilled in one phrase 'you shall love your neighbor as yourself'" (Gal 5:14) and "owe no one anything except to love each other because the person who loves others has fulfilled the law. For the commands 'you will not commit adultery,' 'you will not murder,' 'you will not steal,' 'you will not covet,' and whatever other command, is summed up in this one phrase, 'you will love your neighbor as yourself'" (Rom 13:8–9). If he really meant that Jesus'

Appendix

followers were not under law, why did Paul assert the law? He quotes "love your neighbor as yourself," which is a commandment from the law (Lev 19:12). And why did he try to convince anyone in the churches in Rome or Galatia that this commandment summed up the others? If they were no longer under law, why would that matter?

What is more, Paul did think that Christians have to obey at least some of the commands in the law. He says neither adulterers nor thieves will enter the kingdom of God (1 Cor 6:9–10), so he expected Christians to obey the seventh and eighth commandments (Exod 20:14–15). He identifies idolatry as a work of the sinful flesh and so expects Christians to obey the command not to make or worship any idol (Exod 20:4–6). He quotes "the law of Moses" to teach the Corinthian church how to behave (1 Cor 9:8–14). Paul's attitude to the law cannot have been that his churches were no longer expected to live in accordance with any of the commands of the law. He clearly expected them to live at least some of them out. So, we are presented with the puzzle of how Paul could say on the one hand that his congregations were no longer under the law and on the other hand that they were to obey certain commands from the law (which must have had some authority for Paul, because he quotes it as authoritative).

I think the answer lies in Paul seeing the law as finding its fulfillment in Christ: "for Christ is the end of the law for righteousness for everyone who believes" (Rom 10:4); "the law was our teacher until Christ came, with the result that we are justified by faith" (Gal 3:24). I have no doubt that Paul teaches that we are justified by faith. I simply note that he also teaches that this leads to renewed lives of holiness: "do not present your body parts to [the power of] sin as weapons for unrighteous living, but present yourselves to God as those alive from the dead and present your body parts to God as weapons for righteous living" (Rom 6:13). We are made righteous by Christ, so we must live righteous lives. But the law is no longer our teacher showing us how to be holy. Paul believes that *Jesus* teaches us righteousness: "for surely you have heard him and have been taught by him" (Eph 4:21). Paul notes that Jesus conquered sin by living a sinless life, thus paving the way for teaching us to live holy lives in him: "[Jesus] condemned [the power of] sin in the flesh, so that the commandment of the law might be fulfilled in us who walk not according to the [sinful] flesh but according to the Spirit" (Rom 8:3–4). So, Paul sees Jesus as our teacher who enables us to live holy lives.

Thoughts on Jesus, Paul, and the Law

Paul also sees Jesus as the end of the law. I freely acknowledge that the meaning of this phrase is much disputed. However, given that Paul clearly thinks that believers are not under the law anymore but are still bound to obey some of its commandments, I cannot help but read Paul as following Jesus' own teaching that Jesus is the final interpreter of the Torah—and that Paul assumes that his gentile congregations only have to follow Jesus' teachings (as if the temple had already been destroyed and so the whole Torah no longer applied). This would explain why Paul assumes gentile Christians must obey certain commandments in the Torah (because Jesus did the same), why certain of the commandments are no longer binding on them (because they had been loosed and only Jesus' teachings apply), and why the Torah was still an authority to cite (because Jesus gave the final interpretation of the law, he did not do away with the law).

There are good grounds for reading Paul this way. Paul talks about being subject to the "law of Christ" himself (1 Cor 9:21) and "the law of Christ" being something that believers must fulfill (Gal 6:2). He speaks too of believers who were once slaves of sin now being obedient to the tradition of teaching to which they have been handed over (Rom 6:17)—this tradition of teaching being the teaching of Jesus. We know Paul taught believers to obey the teachings of Jesus as he quotes the command of Jesus on marriage and divorce (1 Cor 7:10–11). Interestingly, Paul says "to those without the law, I became as one without the law (but I am not without the law of God but I am under the law of Christ) so that I might win those without the law" (1 Cor 9:21). He says he became like the gentiles (i.e., without the law) to win them to Christ. However, he qualifies his statement about his becoming as one without the law. He makes it very clear that he was not without the law of God because he was under the law of Christ. In other words, he did not follow the whole of the Torah (like the Jewish Christians in Judea were bound to do until the destruction of the temple), but he did follow the law of Christ (i.e., Jesus' teachings, his final interpretation of the law). He also identifies Jesus' final interpretation of the law as the law of God—just as Jesus does in the Gospel of Matthew where he refers to "my yoke" (Matt 11:29).

If there is any evidence that Paul acted and thought as if the Jerusalem temple had already been destroyed (which physically it had not while he was writing his letters), then it makes sense that he would write as though only Jesus' final interpretation of the law, not the whole law, applies. Paul writes to gentile audiences and makes no effort to win them to the form

Appendix

of Judaism that centers on the land, the temple, and the whole Torah. The Gospels suggest that Jesus had already taught that he would destroy the temple and replace it with another—referring to his body (John 2:19–21; cf. Matt 26:61; Mark 14:58). Paul talks of Christians belonging to the body of Christ. He talks of their body as the temple of the Holy Spirit (1 Cor 6:15, 19) and elsewhere refers to the church as "God's temple" (1 Cor 3:16–17). Paul seems to inherit a tradition that makes the following moves: Christ is the temple of God; Christians are members of the body of Christ; Christians are the temple of God. The Gospels record a tradition that makes the following moves: the temple will be destroyed; Jesus will replace it with the temple of his body. Paul's own theology of the church as temple suggests he knew this tradition and so conducts his mission to the gentiles as if the temple has already been destroyed.

Putting steps one to three together, we reach the following conclusion: that Jesus taught that the temple would be destroyed within a generation, and that parts of the law would disappear with it. Until that time, his Jewish followers were to obey the whole law. After that time, they were only to obey his teachings as they never pass away. Paul conducted his mission to the gentiles as if the temple had already been destroyed. Therefore, he taught them that they were not to obey the whole Torah but only the teachings of Jesus which were now God's law.

Step four: Jewish believers in Galatia tried to get gentiles to obey the wrong teaching

When Paul talks about freedom from the law, he is not talking about the freedom to choose to behave in whatever way seems most loving to the individual believer or church community. (Paul does not teach situation ethics.) For example, he does say "for the whole law is fulfilled in one phrase 'you shall love your neighbor as yourself'" (Gal 5:14) but he also prohibits certain forms of behaving in the same letter: for example, "sexual immorality, impurity, debauchery, idolatry, magic, enmities, strife, jealousy, rages, rivalries, disunities, factionalism, envies, bouts of drunkenness, revelries, and stuff like that" (Gal 5:19–21). In this list alone, he agrees with at least one of the ten commandments because he forbids idolatry (Exod 20:4–6), stating that those who engage in it will not inherit the kingdom of God (Gal 5:21). Paul prescribes certain kinds of behavior and condemns others. He does not leave either individual Christians or even churches to decide what actions are morally permissible.

In the letter to the Galatians, Paul demonstrates his expectation that gentile believers should fulfill the law of Christ (Gal 6:2). Interestingly, the context of his encouragement that believers fulfill the law of Christ is his injunction that they bear each other's burdens. Burdens might refer to life's challenges, but as we have seen, it can refer to interpretations of the law. Jesus commanded his disciples to teach all the nations (all the gentiles) to obey his commands, and to do so lovingly, gently, and with integrity—in the same way as Jesus does. I find it difficult not to read this injunction to bear each other's burdens as referring to helping each other to follow Christ and live out his teachings. However, Paul does not teach the Galatians to try to obey the whole Torah. Indeed, he scolds them for trying to do this (Gal 3:1–5).

What seems to be happening in the Galatian church is that Christians from Judea are trying to get the gentile Galatian believers to follow the gospel Jesus preached to the Jews in Judea. Note that Paul distinguishes between the gospel for the circumcised and the gospel for the uncircumcised (Gal 2:7). The church leaders in Jerusalem made a deal with Paul that they all preach the gospel in the appropriate way to the relevant people. However, some from James (i.e., Christians from the Jerusalem church) started to expect obedience to the whole Torah from gentiles (Gal 2:11–14). The situation in Galatia is that there are Christians in Judea who observe the whole Torah trying to teach Paul's converts to obey the whole Torah. Paul does not think they should and tells them as much. However, he clearly does expect them to live in accordance with some of the law, and certainly to fulfill the law of Christ. What is going on?

The situation is easily explained if the reconstruction of the situation in steps one to three is accepted. Jesus preached to his fellow Jews that the law remained in force until the temple was destroyed. At that time, some of the commands would be loosed. Paul engaged in the gentile mission as if the temple had already been destroyed. He taught his converts that they only had to obey the teachings of Jesus, the "law of Christ." (Note: Matthew records Jesus telling his disciples to teach all the gentile nations to obey all *he had commanded*, not the whole Torah [Matt 28:18–20]). Jews in Jerusalem, probably including James himself, were worried that Paul was jumping the gun. The temple had not yet been destroyed, yet Paul was acting as if it had. How could the gentiles be saved if they lived in disobedience to Jesus?

Appendix

Somebody needed to act on this, and so they did and tried to correct Paul. Sparks flew.[9]

Step five: Jesus' commands remain valid for all Christians for all time

The important thing to note for our purposes is that neither James and his party, nor Paul and his, would for one minute assume that disobedience to the teachings of Jesus was an option. The tradition in the Gospels records Jesus as saying that his words would never pass away. Paul regarded the law of Christ as binding on him, and on the gentile believers. The question at the heart of the debate about freedom from the law was not freedom from all moral commands, or even freedom from all but the love commands, *but whether gentile Christians should obey the whole Torah before the destruction of the temple or only the teaching of Jesus. Both sides of the debate expected that all believers would live according to the teachings of Jesus, precisely because his teachings will never pass away. They stand for all time.*

We began this brief sketch of my thoughts on Jesus, Paul, and the law with the question: which commands of the Torah still ought to be obeyed? My answer has to be "certainly not all of them" and "equally certainly the teachings of Jesus." Contemporary Christians cannot be under any obligation to obey all the commands of Torah because "heaven and earth" have passed away in the destruction of the temple. That happened in AD 70. At that time, many commands of the Torah were loosed. No Christian is under any obligation to live in obedience to any of these loosed commands. However, "heaven and earth" may have passed away but Jesus' words will never pass away. Therefore, all Christians are called to obey the teachings of Jesus and to teach others to do the same, in love, gentleness, and grace.

Given all this, we have clear direction for issues on which Jesus spoke. This does not necessarily make the task of Christian ethics easy, as Jesus' ethical teaching is often remarkably challenging. However, the purpose of this book has been to highlight that the Jesus who presents these challenges in his teaching promises to be present with his disciples helping them to

---

9. Some may note resemblances between my argument here and the thinking of Crispin Fletcher-Louis ("Destruction of the Temple"). This is not accidental. I am indebted to Crispin. I simply reconstruct the same basic idea a bit differently and suggest that this helps to explain Paul and the law, and his relationship with the Jerusalem church.

Thoughts on Jesus, Paul, and the Law

learn to obey his commands—not least in a community of grace. Nevertheless, I am fully aware that this does not necessarily provide much guidance for how we are to act on contested issues on which Jesus did not speak directly, at least as far as we can see on what we think of as a plain reading of the text. Here there are complexities involved in trying to recover exactly which commands might have been loosed and which ones Jesus might expect his followers to obey today. I am under no illusion that my broad outline presented above solves all the problems. It most certainly does not.

However, study of the Gospel narratives provides us with pointers that might help us understand the mind of Christ on such contested matters: the way Jesus does theology and the foundations of his theology; the cultural background of his sayings, which can help us to hear what original hearers heard (but might be lost to us); the ethical implications of his attitudes and assumptions; and the ethical implications of his actions. I do not want to explore these here as they are really the subject of another book. This one has really been about two things: helping readers lost in the quagmires of "Christian hippiedom" (as one reader of the draft manuscript put it) and the myths of "love instead of legalism" to hear the voice of Jesus more clearly; and enabling contemporary Christians to recover the wonderful truth that Jesus' teaching ministry continues today as we meet with him and learn from him how to live his way. My hope has been that in exploring what Matthew tells us of Jesus teachings, we might recover the mind of Christ with the assurance that it remains his mind for all time—and that listening to his voice and obeying his commands we might find ourselves living out the lives of joyful obedience into which he calls us.

Bibliography

Adams, Edward. *The Stars will Fall from Heaven: Cosmic Catastrophe in the New Testament and Its World*. Library of New Testament Studies 347. London: T. & T. Clark, 2007.
Albright, W. F., and C. S. Mann. *Matthew*. Anchor Bible 26. New York: Doubleday, 1971.
Allison, Dale C. *James*. International Critical Commentary. London: Bloomsbury, 2013.
———. *Jesus of Nazareth: Millenarian Prophet*. Minneapolis: Fortress, 1998.
———. *The New Moses: A Matthean Typology*. Minneapolis: Fortress, 1993.
Angel, Andrew R. *Angels: Ancient Whispers of Another World*. Eugene, OR: Cascade, 2012.
———. *Chaos and the Son of Man: The Hebrew Chaoskampf Tradition in the Period 515 BCE to 200 CE*. Library of Second Temple Studies 60. London: T. & T. Clark, 2006.
———. "God Talk and Men's Talk: Jesus, Tarfon and Ishmael in Dialogue." In *Judaism, Jewish Identities and the Gospel Tradition*, edited by James G. Crossley, 95–117. London: Equinox, 2010.
———. "Inquiring into an *Inclusio*—On Judgment and Love in Matthew." *Journal of Theological Studies* 60 (2009) 527–30.
Bacon, Benjamin W. *Studies in Matthew*. 1930. Reprint, New Dehli: Isha, 2013.
Barrett, C. K. *The Gospel according to St John: An Introduction with Commentary and Notes on the Greek Text*. 2nd ed. London: SPCK, 1978.
Bauckham, Richard. *Jesus and the God of Israel: "God Crucified" and Other Studies on the New Testament's Christology of Divine Identity*. Milton Keynes, UK: Paternoster, 2008.
Bell, Rob. *Love Wins*. London: Collins, 2011.
Best, Ernest. *A Critical and Exegetical Commentary on Ephesians*. International Critical Commentary. London: T. & T. Clark, 1998.
Betz, Hans Dieter. *The Sermon on the Mount: A Commentary on the Sermon on the Mount, including the Sermon on the Plain (Matthew 5:3—7:27 and Luke 6:20-49)*. Hermeneia. Minneapolis: Fortress, 1995.
Brandon, S. G. F. "The Date of the Markan Gospel." *New Testament Studies* 7 (1960–61) 126–41.
Bultmann, Rudolph. *The History of the Synoptic Tradition*. Translated by John Marsh. Oxford: Blackwell, 1972.

Bibliography

Byrskog, Samuel. *Jesus the Only Teacher: Didactic Authority and Transmission in Ancient Israel, Ancient Judaism and the Matthean Community.* Coniectanea Biblica New Testament Series 24. Stockholm: Almqvist & Wiksell, 1994.

Calvin, John. *Commentary on a Harmony of the Evangelists of Matthew, Mark, and Luke: volume 1.* Translated by William Pringle. Grand Rapids: Baker, 2009.

Carson, D. A. *The Gospel according to John.* Pillar New Testament Commentary. Leicester, UK: Apollos, 1991.

Collins, Adela Yarbro. *Mark.* Hermeneia. Minneapolis: Fortress, 2007.

Collins, John. "Sibylline Oracles." In *The Old Testament Pseudepigrapha: Apocalyptic Literature and Testaments,* edited by James H. Charlesworth, 1:317–472. London: Darton, Longman and Todd, 1983.

Collins, John, and Adela Yarbro Collins. *King and Messiah as Son of God: Divine, Human and Messianic Figures in Biblical and Related Literature.* Grand Rapids: Eerdmans, 2008.

Crossley, James G. *The Date of Mark's Gospel: Insight from the Law in Earliest Christianity.* Journal for the Study of the New Testament Supplement Series 266. London: T. & T. Clark, 2004.

Davies, W. D., and Dale C. Allison. *A Critical and Exegetical Commentary on the Gospel according to Saint Matthew, volume I: I–VII.* International Critical Commentary. London: T. & T. Clark, 2000.

———. *A Critical and Exegetical Commentary on the Gospel according to Saint Matthew, volume II: VIII–XVIII.* International Critical Commentary. London: T. & T. Clark, 1991.

———. *A Critical and Exegetical Commentary on the Gospel according to Saint Matthew, volume III: XIX–XXVIII.* 2nd ed. International Critical Commentary. London: T. & T. Clark, 2004.

Dibelius, Martin. *James.* Revised by Heinrich Greeven. Translated by Michael A. Williams. 11th ed. Hermeneia. Philadelphia: Fortress, 1975.

Dibelius, Martin, and Hans Conzelmann. *The Pastoral Epistles.* Translated by Philip Buttolph and Adela Yarbro. Hermeneia. Philadelphia: Fortress, 1972.

Dunn, James D. G. *Jesus Remembered.* Christianity in the Making, volume 1. Grand Rapids: Eerdmans, 2003.

Durham, John I. *Exodus.* Word Biblical Commentary 3. Waco, TX: Word, 1987.

Filson, Floyd V. *A Commentary on the Gospel according to Saint Matthew.* Black's New Testament Commentary. London: Black, 1960.

Fitzmyer, Joseph A. *The Acts of the Apostles.* Anchor Bible 31. New York: Doubleday, 1998.

———. *First Corinthians.* Anchor Yale Bible 32. New Haven: Yale University Press, 2008.

———. *Romans.* Anchor Bible 33. New York: Doubleday, 1993.

———. *To Advance the Gospel: New Testament Studies.* 2nd ed. Grand Rapids: Eerdmans, 1998.

———. *Tobit.* Commentaries on Early Jewish Literature. Berlin: de Gruyter, 2003.

Crispin H. T. Fletcher-Louis. "The Destruction of the Temple and the Relativization of the Old Covenant: Mark 13:31 and Matthew 5:18." In *The Reader Must Understand: Eschatology in Bible and Theology,* edited by Kent E. Brower and Mark W. Elliott, 145–69. Leicester, UK: Apollos, 1997.

Fox, Michael V. *Proverbs 1–9.* Anchor Bible 18A. New York: Doubleday, 2000.

France, R. T. *The Gospel of Matthew.* New International Commentary on the New Testament. Grand Rapids: Eerdmans, 2007.

Bibliography

Green, Michael. *The Message of Matthew*. The Bible Speaks Today. Leicester, UK: Inter-Varsity Press, 2000.

Gundry, R. H. *Matthew: A Commentary on His Handbook for a Mixed Church under Persecution*. 2nd ed. Grand Rapids: Eerdmans, 1994.

Hagner, Donald A. *Matthew 1-13*. Word Biblical Commentary. Dallas: Word, 1993.

———. *Matthew 14-28*. Word Biblical Commentary 33B. Dallas: Word, 1995.

Hare, Douglas, R. A. *Matthew*. Interpretation. Louisville: Westminster John Knox, 2009.

Harrington, Daniel J. *The Gospel of Matthew*. Sacra Pagina 1. Collegeville, MN: Liturgical, 1991.

Hays, Richard B. *Echoes of Scripture in the Gospels*. Waco, TX: Baylor University Press, 2016.

Hoehner, Harold W. *Ephesians: An Exegetical Commentary*. Grand Rapids: Baker Academic, 2002.

Hooker, Morna D. *The Gospel according to St Mark*. Black's New Testament Commentaries. London: Continuum, 1991.

Johnson, Luke Timothy. *The First and Second Letters to Timothy*. Anchor Bible 35A. New York: Doubleday, 2001.

———. *The Letter of James*. Anchor Bible 37A. New York: Doubleday, 1995.

Kingsbury, Jack D. *Matthew as Story*. Philadelphia: Fortress, 1986.

———. *Matthew: Structure, Christology, Kingdom*. Philadelphia: Fortress, 1979.

Kittel, Gerhard, and Gerhard Friedrich, eds. *Theological Dictionary of the New Testament*. Translated by Geoffrey W. Bromiley. 10 vols. Grand Rapids: Eerdmans, 1964-76.

Levine, Baruch A. *Leviticus 1-20*. Anchor Yale Bible 4A. New Haven: Yale University Press, 1993.

Luz, Ulrich. *Matthew 1-7*. Translated by James E. Crouch. Hermeneia. Minneapolis: Fortress, 2007.

———. *Matthew 8-20*. Translated by James E. Crouch. Hermeneia. Minneapolis: Augsburg Fortress, 2001.

———. *Matthew 21-28*. Translated by James E. Crouch. Hermeneia. Minneapolis: Augsburg Fortress, 2005.

Malherbe, Abraham J. *The Letters to the Thessalonians*. Anchor Yale Bible 32B. New Haven: Yale University Press, 2000.

Marcus, Joel. *Mark 1-8*. Anchor Bible 27. New Haven: Yale University Press, 2000.

Marshall, I. Howard. *A Critical and Exegetical Commentary on the Pastoral Epistles*. International Critical Commentary. London: T. & T. Clark, 1999.

MacIntyre, Alasdair. "God and the Theologians." In *The Honest to God Debate*, edited by John A. T. Robinson and David L. Edwards, 215-28. London: SCM, 1963.

McL. Wilson, Robert. *A Critical and Exegetical Commentary on Colossians and Philemon*. International Critical Commentary. London: T. & T. Clark, 2005.

Meier, John P. *A Marginal Jew, Rethinking the Historical Jesus, volume I: The Roots of the Problem and the Person*. Anchor Bible Reference Library. New York: Doubleday, 1991.

———. *A Marginal Jew, Rethinking the Historical Jesus, volume II: Mentor, Message and Miracles*. Anchor Bible Reference Library. New York: Doubleday, 1994.

———. *A Marginal Jew, Rethinking the Historical Jesus, volume III: Companions and Competitors*. Anchor Yale Bible Reference Library. New Haven: Yale University Press, 2001.

Bibliography

———. *A Marginal Jew, Rethinking the Historical Jesus, volume IV: Law and Love.* Anchor Yale Bible Reference Library. New Haven: Yale University Press, 2009.

———. *A Marginal Jew, Rethinking the Historical Jesus, volume V: Probing the Authenticity of the Parables.* Anchor Yale Bible Reference Library. New Haven: Yale University Press, 2016.

Meyer, Ben F. *The Aims of Jesus.* London: SCM, 1979.

Milgrom, Jacob. *Leviticus 1–16.* Anchor Bible 3. New York: Doubleday, 1991.

———. *Leviticus 17–22.* Anchor Bible 3A. New Haven: Yale University Press, 2000.

———. *Leviticus 23–27.* Anchor Bible 3B. New Haven: Yale University Press, 2001.

Moo, Douglas J. *The Epistle to the Romans.* New International Commentary on the New Testament. Grand Rapids: Eerdmans, 1996.

———. *The Letters to the Colossians and to Philemon.* Pillar New Testament Commentary. Grand Rapids: Eerdmans, 2008.

Morris, Leon. *The Gospel according to Matthew.* Pillar New Testament Commentary. Grand Rapids: Eerdmans, 1992.

Murphy O'Connor, J. "Teacher of Righteousness." In *The Anchor Bible Dictionary*, edited by David N. Freedman, 6:340–41. New Haven, Yale University Press, 2007.

Neill, Stephen, and N. T. Wright. *The Interpretation of the New Testament 1861–1986.* 2nd ed. Oxford: Oxford University Press, 1988.

Niebuhr, H. Richard. *Christ and Culture.* New York: Harper & Brothers, 1951.

Neusner, Jacob. *From Politics to Piety: The Emergence of Pharisaic Judaism.* Englewood Cliffs, NJ: Prentice Hall, 1973.

———. *The Mishnah: A New Translation.* New Haven: Yale University Press, 1988.

Newman, Carey C., ed. *Jesus and the Restoration of Israel: A Critical Assessment of N. T. Wright's Jesus and the Victory of God.* Downers Grove, IL: InterVarsity Press, 1999.

Nickelsburg, George W. E. *1 Enoch 1: A Commentary on the Book of 1 Enoch, Chapters 1–36; 81–108.* Hermeneia. Minneapolis: Fortress, 2001.

Nickelsburg, George W. E., and James C. VanderKam. *1 Enoch: A New Translation.* Minneapolis: Fortress, 2004.

Nolland, John. *The Gospel of Matthew.* New International Greek Testament Commentary. Grand Rapids: Eerdmans, 2005.

O'Brien, Peter T. *The Letter to the Ephesians.* Pillar New Testament Commentary. Grand Rapids: Eerdmans, 1999.

Propp, William H. *Exodus 19–40.* Anchor Bible 2A. New York: Doubleday, 2006.

Reynolds, Benjamin E. *The Son of Man Problem: Critical Readings.* Critical Readings in Biblical Studies. London: T. & T. Clark, 2018.

Richard, Earl J. *First and Second Thessalonians.* Sacra Pagina 11. Collegeville, MN: Liturgical, 2007.

Robinson, John A. T. *Honest to God.* London: SCM, 1963.

Saldarini, Anthony J. "Pharisees." In *The Anchor Bible Dictionary*, edited by David N. Freedman, 5:289–303. New Haven: Yale University Press, 2007.

Sanders, E. P. *Jesus and Judaism.* London: SCM, 1985.

———. "Law in Judaism of the NT Period." In *The Anchor Bible Dictionary*, edited by David N. Freedman, 4:254–65. New Haven: Yale University Press, 2007

Schweitzer, Albert. *The Quest for the Historical Jesus: A Critical Study of its Progress from Reimarus to Wrede.* Translated by W. Montgomery. London: A & C Black, 1954.

Selbourne, David. *The Principle of Duty: An Essay on the Foundations of the Civic Order.* London: Sinclair-Stevenson, 1994.

Bibliography

Skehan, Patrick W., and Alexander A. Di Lella. *The Wisdom of Ben Sira*. Anchor Bible 39. New York: Doubleday, 1987.

Stein, Robert H. *Jesus, the Temple and the Coming of the Son of Man: A Commentary on Mark 13*. Downers Grove, IL: InterVarsity Press, 2014.

Talbert, Charles H. *Matthew*. Paideia Commentaries on the New Testament. Grand Rapids: Baker Academic, 2010.

Tchividjian, Tullian. *Jesus + Nothing = Everything*. Wheaton, IL: Crossway, 2011.

The Apostolic Fathers. Translated by Bart D. Ehrman. 2 vols. LCL. Cambridge: Harvard University Press, 2003.

Thiselton, Anthony C. *The First Epistle to the Corinthians*. New International Greek Testament Commentary. Grand Rapids: Eerdmans, 2000.

Towner, Philip H. *The Letters to Timothy and Titus*. New International Commentary on the New Testament. Grand Rapids: Eerdmans, 2006.

Turner, David L. *Matthew*. Baker Exegetical Commentary on the New Testament. Grand Rapids: Baker Academic, 2008.

Wenham, G. J. "Matthew and Divorce: An Old Crux Revisited." *Journal for the Study of the New Testament* 22 (1984) 95–107.

Williamson, H. G. M. *Ezra, Nehemiah*. Word Biblical Commentary 16. Waco, TX: Word, 1985.

Witherington, Ben. *The Jesus Quest: The Third Search for the Jew of Nazareth*. 2nd ed. Downers Grove, IL: InterVarsity Press, 1997.

Wright, N. T. *Jesus and the Victory of God*. Christian Origins and the Question of God, volume 2. London: SPCK, 1996.

———. *The New Testament and the People of God*. Christian Origins and the Question of God, volume 1. London: SPCK, 1992.

———. *Paul and the Faithfulness of God*. Christian Origins and the Question of God, volume 4. London: SPCK, 2013.

———. *The Resurrection of the Son of God*. Christian Origins and the Question of God, volume 3. London: SPCK, 2003.

Yancey, Philip. *The Jesus I Never Knew*. Grand Rapids: Zondervan, 1995.

Index of Ancient Sources

Old Testament

Genesis

	17, 29, 55
1	17
1:27	17, 54
2:24	17, 54

Exodus

	17, 28, 29
1:15–16	28
2:15	28
4:19	28
10:3	27
19:10–15	42
20:1—31:18	27
20:3–6	40
20:7	40
20:12	40, 48, 50, 62
20:12–16	67
20:13	40, 52
20:14	40, 53
20:14–15	126
20:15	40
20:16	40
21:17	50
21:24	58
21:26–27	58
22:10	57
29:19–21	46
30:11–16	66
34:21	46

Leviticus

	17, 29
4:1–35	65
4:2	65
5:1	65
5:1–13	65
5:3	64, 65
5:4	56
6:24–30	46
11	50, 51
14:1–32	64
16	69
16:1–34	45
18:6–18	55
19:9–10	61
19:12	56
19:18	126
22:4	46
24:5–9	47
24:8–9	47
24:20	58
27:2	56
27:30	68

Numbers

	17, 29, 56
5:2	46
5:19–22	57
6:2	56

Index of Ancient Sources

Numbers (continued)

15:30–31	43
15:38–39	65
28:9–10	47
30:3–15	56

Deuteronomy

	117, 29, 30, 56, 106
1:1—30:20	27
5:12–15	30
5:16	48, 50, 62
5:16–20	67
5:17	52
5:18	53
6:5	67
11:18–21	30
13:1–11	48
14:22	61, 68
15:11	67
17:14–20	33
19:15	106
19:16–21	106
19:21	58
20:10–18	62
22:12	65
23:21–23	56
23:22	57
24	56
24:1	54
24:1–4	17, 54, 55
24:19–22	61
28:1—29:1	31
31:1	30
31:9–13	32
33:9	48
34	17
34:1–4	27

2 Kings

21:1–18	33
Ezra	28
3:2	28
7:6	28

Nehemiah

	28

1:7–9	28
8:1	28
8:1–18	32
8:14	28
9:14	28
10:29	28
13:1	28

Psalms

	25, 29
50:14	56
96	25
97	25
99	25

Proverbs

	61
6:10–11	61
10:4	61
14:23	61
20:13	61
23:20–21	61
24:33–34	61
28:19	61
Isaiah	15, 20
7:14	20
29:13	50
66:22–24	15

Jeremiah

5:5	78
18:20	16

Lamentations

3:31–33	104

Ezekiel

14:3	16
14:4	16
14:7	16
18:30	16
43:11	16
44:12	16

Daniel

	44, 90, 123, 124

Index of Ancient Sources

6:13	16
7	44, 90
7:9–14	44
7:13–14	44, 90

Hosea

6:6	45

Micah

7:6	49

Zechariah

8:17	56

Apocrypha

Tobit

	61
4:13	61

Wisdom of Solomon

3:4	16
11:13	16
12:15	16
14:10	16
16:2	16
16:9	16
16:24	16
18:11	16
19:4	16

Sirach

	61
45:6–7	32
45:17	32

2 Maccabees

4:38	16
6:14	16
7:1–40	102
7:9	102
7:11	103
7:14	102
7:23	102
7:29	102

3 Maccabees

1:3	16
3:26	16
7:3	16
7:10	16

4 Maccabees

8:9	16

New Testament

Matthew

7, 9–11, 14, 17–21, 27–30, 34, 37–44, 46, 49–52, 59, 66, 68–69, 73–75, 80–81, 90, 97–98, 107, 119–125, 127, 129, 131

1:18–21	28
1:18–22	20
1:21	20, 28
1:22–23	20
1:23	18, 44, 49
2:1–8	28
2:3	43
2:13–14	28
2:16	28
2:19–20	28
2:23	108
3:2	17
3:5	43
3:6	73
3:7	73
3:7–12	17
3:11	73
3:13–17	65
3:15	65
4:10	40
4:17	17, 25, 69, 97
4:23	26
5:1	76
5:1—7:27	29
5:11–12	31
5:17	81, 96
5:17–20	37, 41
5:19	39, 95, 122
5:20	52, 62
5:21	52
5:21–22	18, 40, 52
5:21–26	52, 61

Index of Ancient Sources

Matthew (continued)

5:21–30	56
5:21–48	52
5:22	15, 17, 22, 53
5:23–26	53
5:27–30	18, 40, 53
5:29–30	9, 17
5:31	52
5:31–32	52, 54
5:32	55
5:33	56
5:33–34	52
5:33–37	40, 56–57
5:38–39	52
5:38–42	57
5:39	59
5:39–42	59
5:40	60
5:41	60
5:43–44	52
5:43–48	61
5:46	107
5:47	62, 107
6:4	17
6:6	17
6:7	107
6:14–15	110
6:18	17
6:32	107
7:1	17, 77
7:1–2	77
7:1–5	75, 96
7:2	96
7:3–5	77
7:21–23	9, 19, 81
7:22–23	23
7:23	95, 97
7:24	94
7:24–27	23, 27, 31
7:26	94
7:28	29
7:28–29	32
8:1–4	64
8:4	67, 95
8:11–12	17
8:12	11
8:20	90
8:22	62
9:2	44
9:2–8	43
9:3	43
9:6	44
9:9	107
9:10	107
9:11	107
9:13	45
9:14	45
9:20–22	45
9:25	46
9:26	90
10:5–42	29
10:15	17
10:23	90
10:34–39	49
10:42	18
11:1	29
11:13	63
11:18	45
11:19	90, 107
11:20–24	17
11:28–30	77, 80
11:29	38, 86, 95, 101, 120, 127
12:1–2	46
12:4	47
12:6–7	47
12:8	47, 90
12:9	41
12:9–14	47
12:18–21	107
12:32	15, 90
12:36–37	18
12:40	90
12:46–50	34, 48
12:50	94
13:1–52	29
13:24–30	17
13:36–43	17
13:37	90
13:39	15, 21
13:40	15, 97
13:40–42	73
13:40–43	21
13:41	90
13:41–42	31
13:42	11

Index of Ancient Sources

13:47–49	17	19:16–22	67
13:47–50	25	19:16–30	10, 15
13:49	15, 97	19:17	67
13:49–50	21, 73	19:18	40
13:50	11	19:19	40
13:53	29	19:22	118
14:35–36	65	19:24–25	18
15:2	49	19:25	118
15:3	50, 95	19:26	118
15:3–9	69	19:27–30	18, 31
15:4–9	40	19:28	90
15:11	50	19:29	49
15:20	51	20:18	90
16:11–12	43	20:20–23	99
16:13	90	20:25	107
16:24–27	70	20:28	40, 90
16:27	72, 90	21:28–31	70
16:27–28	90	21:31	70
17:9	90	21:31–32	107
17:12	90	21:33–41	17
17:22	90	22:1–14	10, 17
17:24–27	66	22:13	11
17:27	66	22:15–22	63
18	53	22:23–32	102
18:1–5	99	22:34–40	32, 67
18:1–14	105	22:37–40	95
18:1–35	29	22:40	67
18:3	100	23:2–3	42–43
18:4	100	23:4	79–80
18:5	100	23:8	34, 74–75, 77, 120
18:6	100	23:8–10	34
18:6–9	18, 102	23:23	2, 68
18:8	15	24:1–2	67
18:10–14	104	24:1–4	65
18:11	104	24:1–44	18
18:15–18	105	24:1—25:46	29
18:15–20	105, 108	24:3	15, 21, 122
18:15–22	15, 53	24:20	68
18:20	108	24:27	90
18:21–35	105, 109	24:29	39
18:23–35	17	24:29–35	40
19:1	29	24:30	44, 90
19:3	54	24:34–35	39, 124
19:3–9	32, 54	24:35	39, 125
19:4–9	17	24:37	90
19:6	54	24:39	90
19:8	55	24:44	90
19:9	55	24:45–51	17

Index of Ancient Sources

Matthew (continued)

24:51	11
25:1–30	17
25:30	11
25:31	90
25:31–46	10, 13, 18, 40, 124
25:34–40	31
25:41	15
25:46	13, 15–16
26:1	29–30
26:2	90
26:24	10, 90
26:28	40
26:39	65
26:45	90
26:64	90
26:64–66	44
28	90
28:16–20	89, 108
28:18	92
28:18–20	72, 74–75, 90, 107, 129
28:19	73
28:19–20	108
28:20	15, 18, 20, 74, 81, 94–95, 97, 101, 108, 119

Mark

	7, 11, 14, 29, 31–32, 38, 43, 48–51, 69, 119, 122–123
1:9–11	65
1:14–15	69
1:22	32
1:29–31	48
2:7	43
3:4	48
4:19	15
7:1–23	50–51
7:19	51
9:47–48	15
10:17–32	15
10:28–31	31
10:35–37	99
12:28–34	32
12:34	32

Luke

	7, 12, 14, 29–30, 38, 41, 43, 48–49, 119, 121–125
3:21–22	65
4:38–39	48
5:21	43
6:9	48
6:17–49	30
7:33	45
10:25	15
16:8	15
16:19–31	13
18:18–30	15
20:34	15
20:35	15
24:53	41, 67

John

	7, 11–12, 15, 26, 36, 38, 119
1:38	34
6:40	15
8:11	26
12:25	15
14:15	96, 119
17:3	15

Acts

1:6	99
3:1	41
4:21	16
6:13	67
15:10	78

Romans

	5, 83
1:18	82
3:24–25	82
3:25	83
5:1	83
6:17	86, 120, 127
8:1	83
8:38–39	24
11:13–25	83
11:22	6, 24, 83
12:2	98
13:11–12	83

Index of Ancient Sources

14:10	24

1 Corinthians

1:4–9	84
1:8	85
3:16–17	128
6:9	83
6:9–10	126
6:15	128
7:10–11	127
9:8–14	126
9:21	127

2 Corinthians

5:9–10	83

Galatians

	129
2:7	129
2:11–14	129
3:1–5	129
3:2	120
3:11	120
3:24	126
5:1	78
5:14	125, 128
5:18	125
5:19–21	83, 128
5:21	128
6:2	127, 129

Ephesians

	84–85
4:11	75
4:17–21	85
5:3–5	83

Philippians

3:17–19	84

Colossians

	16, 84
1:20	14
1:23	16
3:5–6	84

1 Thessalonians

4:6	84
5:9–10	83

2 Thessalonians

	84
4:14–15	84

1 Timothy

	84
6:13–14	84

2 Timothy

	84
4:14	84

Titus

2:11–13	84

James

	77
3:1	77

1 John

4:18	16

Revelation

3:19	71
3:20	71

Pseudepigrapha

1 Enoch

	15, 29
90:20–27	15

Dead Sea Scrolls

1QS

1:10–11	62

CD

1:9–11	33
11:13–14	47
20:1	33
20:32	33

Index of Ancient Sources

Josephus

Jewish War

2:162	33
7:218	66

Antiquities of the Jews

2:15–16	28
2:205–7	28
2:210–16	28
3:87	48
4:280	58
13:298	33
18:15	33
18:312	66

Against Apion

1:39	29

Philo

Spec. Laws

1:58	48
4:160–67	33

Moses

2:22	46

Rabbinic Literature

Mishnah

m. 'Abot

1:1	31–32, 42
1:1–2:8	31
1:12	32
3:2	108
3:2–3	108
3:3	108
3:5	78

m. B. Qam.

8:6	59

m. Ber.

3:1	62

m. Demai

2:1	68

m. Giṭ

9:3	55
9:10	43, 54

m. Ḥag.

2:2	50

m. Ḥul.

2:5	50

m. Ma'aś

4:5	68

m. Pesaḥ

6:1–6	47

m. Sanh.

7:5	43

m. Ta'an.

2:1	45

Index of Ancient Sources

m. Yad.

| 3:2 | 50 |

m. Yoma

| 8:6 | 47–48 |

Talmud

y. Šabb.

| 7:2 | 46 |

Other rabbinic works

Abot de Rabbi Nathan

| 2 | 42 |
| 15 | 42 |

Apostolic Fathers

Didache

	74, 107
7:1	74
15:3	107

Index of Modern Authors

Ackley, Alfred Henry, 116
Adams, Edward, 40, 123
Albright, W.F., 48
Allison, Dale C., 20, 28, 30, 34, 37–39, 43, 45, 47–48, 52–53, 55–56, 58–60, 62–64, 66–67, 74, 76–80, 90, 99–100, 102–3, 106–8, 110, 120
Angel, Andrew R., 21, 39, 44, 53, 104, 123–24

Bacon, Benjamin W., 30
Barrett, C.K., 26
Bauckham, Richard, 120
Bell, Rob., 12–16
Best, Ernest, 84, 86
Betz, Hans Dieter, 57, 59
Brandon, S.G.F., 48
Bultmann, Rudolph, 51
Byrskog, Samuel, 32

Calvin, John, 10, 40–41
Carson, D.A., 26
Collins, Adela Yarbro., 15, 29, 44
Collins, John J., 15, 44
Conzelmann, Hans, 84
Crossan, John Dominic, 12
Crossley, James G., 46, 48, 50–51, 58, 63, 65, 68

Da Siena, Bianco, 117

Davies, W.D., 20, 28, 30, 34, 37, 39, 43, 54, 47–48, 52–53, 55–56, 58–60, 62–64, 66–67, 74, 76, 78–80, 90, 99, 100, 102–3, 106–8, 110, 120
Dibelius, Martin, 77, 84
Di Lella, Alexander A., 61
Dunn, James D.G., 63
Durham, John I., 59

Ehrman, Bart D., 74

Filson, Floyd V., 43, 50
Fiorenza, Elizabeth Schüssler, 12
Fitzmyer, Joseph A., 55, 61, 82, 85–86, 99
Fletcher-Louis, Crispin H.T., 130
Fox, Michael V., 61
France, R.T., 20, 34, 39–40, 43, 48, 55–57, 60, 65, 73, 78–79, 100, 104

Green, Michael, 48
Gundry, R.H., 29, 43–44, 56, 79, 100

Hagner, Donald A., 48, 50, 55–56, 66, 79, 99–100
Hare, Douglas, R.A., 48–49, 117, 123
Harrington, Daniel J., 43, 48, 55–57, 60, 62, 65–66, 73
Hays, Richard B., 30
Hoehner, Harold W., 85–86
Hooker, Morna D., 51

Index of Modern Authors

Horsley, Richard A., 12

Johnson, Luke Timothy, 77, 84

Kingsbury, Jack D., 66

Levine, Baruch A., 56–57
Luz, Ulrich, 17–21, 34, 38, 48, 56, 60, 66, 79, 100, 106–7

Malherbe, Abraham J., 84
Marcus, Joel, 51
Marshall, I. Howard, 84
MacIntyre, Alasdair, 92
Mann, C.S., 48
McL. Wilson, R., 84
Meier, John P., 33, 38
Meyer, Ben F., 38
Milgrom, Jacob, 56, 65
Moo, Douglas J., 82, 84
Morris, Leon, 46, 48, 56, 65
Murphy-O'Connor, J., 33

Neill, Stephen, 38
Neusner, Jacob, 32, 50
Newman, Carey C., 12
Nickelsburg, George W.E., 15
Nolland, John, 34, 48, 53, 55–57, 60, 66

O'Brien, Peter T., 84

Propp, William H., 57–58

Reynolds, Benjamin E., 122
Richard, Earl J., 84
Robinson, John A.T., 92

Saldarini, Anthony J., 33
Sammis, John H., 116
Sanders, E.P., 12, 32, 38
Schweitzer, Albert, 12
Selbourne, David, 115
Skehan, Patrick W., 61
Stein, Robert H., 123

Talbert, Charles H., 43, 48, 54, 56
Tchividjian, Tullian, 113
Thiselton, Anthony C., 85
Towner, Philip H., 84
Turner, David L., 45, 48, 55–56, 65, 99

VanderKam, James C., 15

Watts, Isaac, 117
Wenham, G.J., 55
Wesley, Charles, 117
Williamson, H.G.M., 28
Witherington, Ben, 12
Wright, N.T., 12, 33, 38, 40, 48, 103, 123

Yancey, Philip, 36